MOUNTAIN

Biking

THE ROARING FORK VALLEY

RICHARD COMPTON

DEDICATION

To the mountains of Colorado,
who give us life and beauty,
and gracefully withstand our endless follies.

PUBLISHED BY

WHO Press
P.O. Box 1920
Aspen, Colorado 81612

Library of Congress Catalog Card Number: 96–60373

ISBN 1-882426-04-5

Printed in the United States of America

Photos by Richard Compton

Cover photo by Richard Compton

Designed and edited by Warren H. Ohlrich

Cover Design by Curt Carpenter

Table of Contents

Introduction   6

Aspen   11

1. Rio Grande Trail 11
2. Smuggler Mountain Road 13
3. Warren Lakes 14
4. Hunter Creek 15
5. Smuggler/Hunter Creek Loop 18
6. Four Corners 19
7. Sunnyside Trail 20
8. Van Horn Park 22
9. Lenado Loop 23
10. Summer Road 25
11. Midnight Mine Road 27
12. Little Annie Road 28
13. Richmond Hill Road 29
14. Taylor Pass 31
15. Pearl Pass Road to Crested Butte 33
16. Lincoln Creek Road 35

Snowmass Village   37

17. Rim Trail 37
18. Elk Camp Road 40
19. High Alpine Road 40
20. Government Trail 41
21. Government Trail West 43
22. Two Creeks Trail 44
23. Anaerobic Nightmare 45

Woody Creek   46

24. Lenado Road 46

25. Larkspur Mountain 48

26. Arbaney-Kittle Trail to Triangle Peak 50

27. Watson Divide Road 53

28. Snowmass Creek Road 54

29. Capitol Creek Road 55

Basalt   56

30. Frying Pan River Road 56

31. Lime Creek Road 59

32. Burnt Mountain Loop 60

33. Hagerman Pass Road 61

34. Sellar Peak Road 64

35. Basalt Bike Path 65

36. East Sopris Creek Road 67

37. West Sopris Creek Road to Dinkle Lake 68

38. Hay Park Trail 69

39. Around the Table 71

El Jebel   75

40. Upper Cattle Creek Road 75

41. Fender Lane 77

42. Crystal Springs/Cattle Creek Loop 77

43. Spring Valley Loop 78

44. Cottonwood Pass Road 79

45. Basalt Mountain Road 81

46. Trail 1909 83

47. Red Table Road 85

48. Ruedi Trail 87

Carbondale/Crystal River Valley   88

49. Thompson Creek Road 88

50. Dry Park Road 90

51. Tall Pines 91

52. Prince Creek Road 93

53. Porcupine Loop 94

54. Crown Trails 94

55. Schofield Pass Road to Crested Butte 97

56. Lead King Basin/Lost Trail Creek 100

57. Ragged Mountain Trail 102

Glenwood Springs   105

58. Glenwood Canyon Bike Path 105

59. Red Mountain Road 107

60. Transfer Trail 109

61. Red Canyon Road 110

62. Lookout Mountain Road 112

63. Boy Scout Trail 113

64. Four Mile Park Road 115

65. Sunlight Peak 117

Introduction

Riding a mountain bike is, by far, the most versatile way of getting around and enjoying the Roaring Fork Valley. Mountain biking offers nearly the same intimacy and quiet as walking, combined with vastly increased mobility. Not even a jeep will take you where a mountain bike can go, and what you lose in speed you more than gain in enjoyment of the countryside. The "cost" of riding a bike, of course, is getting some good exercise—which, in the Rocky Mountains, adds up very quickly. It's possible to take a mountain bike almost anywhere, and it's tempting to forget that there are some places where it's against the law—across private lands where there is no public right-of-way and in all designated Wilderness Areas. While a few may chafe at any restrictions on their freedom of movement, the fact of the matter is, in the Roaring Fork Valley, that little is lost and much is gained by respecting these boundaries.

Mastering the high country roads and trails requires both superb conditioning and expert bike-handling skills but, as with skiing in the wintertime, there are plenty of opportunities for non-fanatics as well. The purpose of this guide is to help you find your way around the byways and backcountry of the Roaring Fork Valley, whatever your abilities and ambitions. For the new or casual rider, it covers the back roads from Aspen and Glenwood; for the more ambitious it contains a selection of challenging rides throughout the valley and beyond. Many riders know one part of the valley intimately—few, if any, know all the riding possibilities. Without attempting to be exhaustive (and exhausting), our goal is to provide everyone with some opportunity to stretch their limits.

The ride descriptions are grouped in relation to the seven major settlements in the Roaring Fork Valley—Aspen, Snowmass Village, Woody Creek, Basalt, El Jebel, Carbondale, and Glenwood Springs. Rides that extend beyond this watershed (to Crested Butte, etc.) are listed according to their place of origin.

Route Descriptions

(example)

5. Smuggler/Hunter Creek Loop

Round Trip: (from town) 7.5 miles, 1-2 hours
Elevation Gain: 1,200'
Difficulty: Intermediate/Advanced, Strenuous
Map: p. 18

Route Number: Reference number for maps and referrals from other route descriptions.

Name: Usually the common name, may also include descriptive or official wording for clarity's sake.

Round Trip: Gives you total distance from and back to place of origin, unless it's a point-to-point ride, in which case it's specified as "One Way." The time estimate ranges from fast-without-stopping to taking your time without dawdling (and assuming you're not in way over your head). If the route description includes two variations, the different distances/times are given with a slash in between them, i.e., 7.5/10 miles, 1-2/2-3 hours

Elevation Gain: Indicates total climbing footage, not the difference between the start and the high point.

Difficulty: Rated for both the skill level (Beginning, Intermediate, Advanced, Expert) and the effort (Easy, Moderate, Strenuous) required. Theoretically, a ride could be both very smooth (Beginning) and very steep (Strenuous). A combined rating (Intermediate/Advanced) means it's mostly intermediate with a few short advanced sections that can be walked without making a chore out of the whole ride.

Map: Indicates page(s) on which map(s) of route are printed.

In the text that follows the header information:

Notes: An overview of the ride—what kind of experience to expect, its attractions and limitations.

Access: Tells you how to get there from one of the hub areas; for the more remote rides it may refer you back to another route description that covers the intervening ground.

Route: A summary describing the main features and distance intervals along the way.

Backcountry Smarts

Once upon a time an experienced mountain biker set out for a late afternoon ride—a 12-mile loop not far from his home, in an area where he had ridden many times before. Only a few miles of the route were new to him, and he had a good map. Unfortunately, the start of the new trail was very obscure, and he and his friend used up half an hour going down a dead-end road (which wasn't on the map) and then searching around for the right trail. The sun was setting but they decided to go for it anyway—it was less than 3 miles, downhill, to the road home. Unfortunately, the trail was very steep and rough, and difficult to ride. They made slow progress and it began to get dark. No problem—they could follow a trail in the dark, even if it was barely there—until it came to a creek, where it split up. None of the fingers appeared to cross the creek, so they followed the most promising one up the side of a hill, carrying, pushing, dragging their bikes through the brush, finding their way with their feet. At the top of the hill the trail disappeared entirely. They contemplated spending the night there, but decided to push on down the other side until they struck the main creek, on the other side of which was the road home.

They found a creek and crossed it, and began following a trail that ran along the other side. After ½ mile it was still running downstream, so the experienced mountain biker decided it was time to leave the trail and bushwhack up to the road. He wanted to check the map to be sure they were doing the right thing, but they didn't have so much as a match between them, let alone a flashlight. So they set off up the hill anyway, through the thistles and the oakbrush, heading for the low point on the horizon where the road went through the hills. An hour later, the gap in the hills was no closer, but they thrashed their way up through one last tangle of brush, because he was sure the road had to be right there.

It wasn't, so they quit for the night, curling up on the rough ground in their shorts and t-shirts. It rained hard that night, all over the county—everywhere except in the little mountain valley where two lost heroes lay shivering in the grass. Which was fortunate, because the creek they had crossed wasn't the main creek, it was the same side creek they had been following in the first place, and the trail they had abandoned was the same one they had started down. They had left it no more than ½ mile before reaching their road home, and struggled valiantly back into the hills, going east instead of south—running parallel to the road they wanted but in the wrong direction and on the wrong side of the elusive main creek.

You can be sure that the next time we got lost in the dark we had headlamps and warm clothes and plenty of snacks, and that neither of those obscure routes are included in this guidebook. Which doesn't let you, dear reader, off the hook. The mere possession of a map or guidebook, or even years of traveling through the mountains, is no insurance against getting lost, getting wet, having a breakdown, or otherwise suffering unforeseen delays and mishaps. The only alternative to simply suffering is to travel prepared.

- Keep your bike well-tuned.
- It's always safer to ride with someone.
- Before you leave, leave a note describing your route and timetable. If you haven't ridden the route before, bring a guidebook or a topographic map for the area. Remember that riding at altitude will slow you down, and the long climbs typical of many rides in this area will wear you out in a hurry.
- Carry a basic repair kit including: spare inner tube and tire irons, tube patch kit, adjustable wrench or wrenches, screwdriver, allen wrench kit, and chain tool. A "combination" tool can save space and weight.
- Take lots of water, a quart per hour is ideal.
- Bring snack food—we always run out of energy sooner than we expect.
- Bring a rain jacket on all but the sunniest, shortest rides. On long or high altitude rides bring an extra warmth layer—fleece works best.
- The best place to carry stuff is in a fanny pack. Your tool kit can go in a seat or frame pouch; bags that sit or hang on a rack get increasingly cumbersome as the going gets rougher.
- Surviving the night: a headlamp or flashlight is essential, as are matches or a lighter, and an emergency space blanket can make a difference when it's cold or nasty.

Summer in the Roaring Fork Valley is generally pleasant, and we can go for days or weeks with hardly a cloud in the sky. It's easy to forget that afternoon thunderstorms are the norm and blue skies can give way to a thunderous downpour in less than an hour, turning dusty trails into a slick, clinging goo that jams between your wheels and brakes. Trying to ride a muddy trail can be as draining and dangerous as the weather. It's also the worst thing you can do to the trail—tearing up the surface and making ruts that accelerate erosion and tempt other riders to widen the trail by going around them. Riding in the mud can be fun, but it's bad form, as is riding in Wilderness Areas. It's unfortunate that a few trails are off limits, but the whole world doesn't need to be a thrill park.

Sharing the mountain roads and trails with others can feel limiting too, but courtesy is in everyone's best interest. Horses, especially, need to be given the right of way. Stop and step off the trail—most horses aren't much bothered by bikes but some will spook and run. Cows and the damage they do to trails are no fun at all. Ranchers, however, are pretty good about sharing access to the backcountry, which is more than can be said for private estates and gated subdivisions. So it's in our self-interest to treat them as allies, as well as being proper and courteous to close gates behind ourselves as we ride through their grazing allotments.

Forest Service Information

Aspen Ranger District
806 W. Hallam
Aspen, CO 81611
(970) 925-3445

Sopris Ranger District
620 Main Street
Carbondale, CO 81623
(970)963-2266

White River National Forest
900 Grand Avenue
Glenwood Springs, CO 81601
(970)945-2521

Acknowledgments

This book has been a labor of love—a love for mountain biking and the Roaring Fork Valley backcountry, a love that many people have shared with me in making this book possible. Thanks first to Barbara Belmont for prompting me and helping me with an earlier guide to the Aspen area. To Lou Dawson—friend, fellow rider and example and supporter in the guidebook writing business. To Ned Ryerson and Chase Harrison for their unflagging enthusiasm and willingness to help. Most of all to Beverly Keifer, for putting up with my riding and writing traumas and constantly pushing me along. And finally to Warren Ohlrich, editor and publisher, for his endless patience and doing all the dirty work.

Aspen

Mountain biking around Aspen is not for the faint of heart and lung. At the high, narrow end of the Roaring Fork Valley, "getting out of town" generally means getting right into the mountains. With the notable exception of the Rio Grande Trail (Route #1), the Aspen area rides all involve a fair amount of climbing. The good news is that most of the rides are on maintained dirt roads—you can get up some steep climbs without facing major technical difficulties.

The whole system of bike paths and routes in and around the city itself are mentioned here only when used as access routes to the featured rides. There are several city bike maps, including "Bike Maps of Aspen," also from WHO Press, which include some of the longer rides in the immediate area. The Aspen Skiing Company is looking at lift access for mountain bikers on Aspen Mountain and Buttermilk; check with the ticket office below the Silver Queen Gondola for current status of these operations. Also check with the Roaring Fork Transit Authority about transporting bikes on the buses around Aspen and the Roaring Fork Valley.

1. Rio Grande Trail

Round Trip: (to Tavern) 15 ½ miles, 1–2 hours
Elevation Gain: (on return trip) 500'
Difficulty: Beginner/Intermediate, Easy/Moderate
Map: pp. 14, 17

Notes: The Rio Grande Trail is named for the Denver and Rio Grande Railroad, which brought the first train into Aspen in 1887. The last 8 miles of track were torn up years ago, and the old railroad bed makes a lovely, wide, gently-graded bike trail between Aspen and Woody Creek—where the inimitable Woody Creek Tavern provides a refreshing break before returning to town. The first 1 ¾ miles have been paved, and are crowded with dog-walkers, joggers listening to their tunes, in-line skaters, and young riders who ought to still be on training wheels—in short, some of the scariest riding around. After passing under the Slaughterhouse Bridge, the trail turns to dirt and gravel for a relaxing, less crowded ride above the Roaring Fork River.

Access: The bike path begins on the north side of Puppy Smith Street by the Aspen Post Office. From the intersection of Mill and Main, go down the hill on North Mill Street to the 3-way stop sign and turn left onto Puppy Smith Street. Stay to the right and pick up the bike path on the far side of the entrance to the small shopping plaza on the north side of the street.

To avoid the traffic on Mill Street, you can take a bike path that begins next to the County Court House on the north end of Galena Street (one block east of Mill). Go down the hill between the youth center and the jail, cross North Spring Street and circle around the playing field to come back to North Mill opposite Puppy Smith Street at the 3-way stop.

The main (unpaved) part of the Rio Grande can also be reached via Cemetery Lane. Go right at the first stop light west of Aspen on Highway 82; the road is suburban for ½ mile, then drops down a fast hill to the river. Cross the bridge and turn left into a small parking area to pick up the trail.

Route: In the first ¼ mile from the post office are a 3-way intersection, two bridges, and a road crossing; once past these interruptions the bike path rolls freely along the Roaring Fork floodplain for 1 ½ miles to Cemetery Lane and the Slaughterhouse Bridge. Twice the path wanders from the railroad bed to follow the river, which adds some variety but also several blind curves—you can't really cut loose and let your bike roll with the terrain. At Cemetery Lane, fork left and under the bridge to continue towards Woody Creek.

The paved path gives way to a wide, graveled trail close to the river with steep, rocky bluffs on either side. After ½ mile the river begins cutting itself a canyon with the trail shelving along one side. About 1 ½ miles below the bridge is Whitehorse Springs—a thin sheet of water cascading down the shale bluff above the trail. Between the springs, afternoon showers, and the clayey soil, this section of the trail is often wet, and the gray mud doesn't like to come out of your clothes. A mile beyond the springs, the trail emerges onto a wide, sage-covered bench and arrows across these flats for 1 ½ miles until it makes a sharp right at the edge of a reclaimed gravel quarry.

Here you can bear left down a moderately rough single track that will take you to Wilton Jaffee Park—a fisherman's parking area by the Woody Creek Bridge. Go through the intersection at the bridge and follow the River Road 1 ¼ miles to the Woody Creek Tavern. An easier, slightly longer, alternative is to keep right at the top of the pit to the W/J Ranch road, turn left through the ranch to McLain Flats Road, and bear left again down the hill to the bridge. On the return trip, you can take the trail or follow the paved road up onto McLain Flats to ride through wide

open fields with a spectacular view of the Elk Mountains, then plunge
back down to the river and the Rio Grande Trail at the Slaughterhouse
Bridge.

2. Smuggler Mountain Road

Round Trip: 3.2 miles, 30–45 minutes
Elevation Gain: 800'
Difficulty: Intermediate, Strenuous
Map: p.17

Notes: Smuggler Mountain Road is the most popular ride in the Aspen
area. It starts at the northeast corner of town (where the most locals live)
and provides a short, hard workout to the "Platform" (a viewpoint
overlooking Aspen) with the option of extending the ride into Hunter
Creek. The Platform offers a splendid view of town and down the valley
to Mount Sopris; watching the sun set behind Sopris on a still summer
evening is enough to wash away all the cares of the day.

Access: From the Mill and Main light in Aspen, go north down Mill Street
to the river. Immediately after crossing the bridge, turn right onto Gibson
Avenue and up a short, steep hill. After cresting the hill, bear left on
South Ave., and at the Y-intersection at Spruce Street stay right on South
Ave. From here you can see the lower switchbacks of the Smuggler
Mountain Road a quarter-mile ahead.

Route: Four tight, steep switchbacks take you past the Smuggler Mine
and up onto the old mining road, which eases off after the next
switchback. After passing an ultramodern house, enjoy another respite
before the climb begins in earnest. Two more switchbacks get you onto
the long cut so visible from town, which takes you through the scrubby
gambel oak forest, across the top of an old mine dump, and all the way
around the front of the mountain. At the end of the cut a gentle curve
takes you back into the spruce/fir forest for a moment before arriving at
the platform turnout on your right. Take a break and enjoy the view
before going back down Smuggler Mountain or taking the
Smuggler/Hunter Creek Loop (see Route #5) which heads into the
woods directly across from the platform. The Smuggler Mountain Road
itself continues back across the face of the mountain for ½ mile before
starting the killer climb up to Warren Lakes (see Route #3).

3. Warren Lakes

Round Trip: (from town) 12 miles, 2–3 hours

Elevation Gain: 2,900'

Difficulty: Advanced, Very strenuous

Map: pp. 14, 17

Notes: Warren Lakes is a hard-core extension of the Smuggler Mountain Road, a test piece for those who pride themselves on their strength and bike handling. The lakes and the adjoining peat bog—an unusual ecosystem for this area—are part of a private inholding presently owned by Vail Associates, which reportedly bought it as an asset to trade for

National Forest land closer to home. If this happens, the area will soon be open to the public and worth even a long push up the hill.

Access: (See Route #2). Follow Smuggler Mountain Road to the platform turnout.

Route: At the Smuggler platform turnout, continue straight ahead for ½ mile of moderate climbing across the side of the mountain. A short, steep pitch leads to a large parking/party area; continue straight ahead into the woods and up some steep switchbacks—the beginning of a mile of hard, often loose, climbing. A large microwave reflector appears on the right soon after the switchbacks end; many people bail out here before the real pain begins. The road goes straight up the mountain for a good ½ mile before topping out and rewarding you with a leisurely, 2-mile cruise through the pine forest to Warren Lakes.

4. Hunter Creek

Round Trip: (from town to Reservoir Bridge) 7 miles, 1–2 hours
Elevation Gain: 950'
Difficulty: Intermediate, Moderate
Map: p. 17

Notes: Hunter Creek is Aspen's back yard; on a summer afternoon dozens of people migrate into the valley, walking, running, bicycling, and generally enjoying the ambiance of a broad, meadowed, glacial valley two miles from downtown. The route described below is the easiest way to get into Hunter Creek Valley, but does involve some pavement riding at the beginning.

Another way into Hunter Creek Valley is over Smuggler Mountain (see Route #5). This option requires some extra climbing, but gets you off the pavement sooner and rewards you with an exciting downhill plunge into the valley. Smuggler is the choice of hardriders and of many people doing a loop through Hunter Creek and back to town (see Route #5). If you're looking for an easier ride or are headed up to Four Corners and beyond, the route up Hunter Creek described here is the logical choice.

Access: From the Mill and Main light in Aspen, go north down Mill Street to the bridge and fork left onto Red Mountain Road. The road goes over a little knoll and crosses Hunter Creek, climbs another short hill, and then begins a brutal, ¼-mile climb up to the ridge of Red Mountain. A short flat leads you to a hairpin turn to the right and an easier climb to Hunter

Creek Road, which drops down to the right at the next (left-hand) hairpin turn, 1.1 miles from the bridge. Turn right onto Hunter Creek Road which traverses across the face of Red Mountain with views of town and up the Roaring Fork River, then turns back into the Hunter Creek drainage. Go around another hairpin turn and up a short hill to the trailhead on the right, which is marked by a sign and section of split-rail fence (1.7 miles from bridge).

Parking: If you want to avoid traffic and the climb up to the trailhead, use the public parking area on Hunter Creek Road . After turning onto Hunter Creek Road, drive .3 miles and turn sharply left into a gravel driveway (signed "Hunter Creek Trail Parking"). From the lot, ride back down the driveway and continue left on Hunter Creek Road to the trailhead.

Route: The first part of the trail follows an old toll road that led to the mines in Hunter Creek Valley and Van Horn Park. After ¼ mile on the level the trail crosses the Benedict Bridge across Hunter Creek and continues to follow the old roadbed up a steep, cobbly hill that soon levels off and smooths out. Once the valley opens up, the trail leaves the road and becomes winding single track, mostly smooth with some rough and tricky spots. Remember that this route is heavily used and keep an eye out for downhill traffic. The valley opens up into meadows at the National Forest boundary; soon thereafter the trail forks. The left fork dips down to the creek and crosses the Tenth Mountain Bridge to a 4-wheel drive road (Hunter Valley Trail) on the other side; the right fork continues as a single track up along the right side of the creek and through the meadows to the Reservoir Bridge.

The single track is more commonly ridden back down the creek, so the easier and more sensible choice is to cross the Tenth Mountain Bridge and bear right onto the road near a tumble-down barn (a left on the road will take you up the north side of the valley to Van Horn Park and Four Corners—see Routes #6 and #8). The road continues for a mile through a long meadow to the Reservoir Bridge, with long vistas up Hunter Creek and back across the Roaring Fork Valley to the Maroon Bells. At the bridge you have several options: turn around and retrace you route; cross the bridge and immediately turn right to go back down the single track; or continue another two miles along on the north side of the creek. Along the north side of the creek the trail climbs and descends two small, short hills, wanders across a large, sloping meadow past several derelict log cabins, and after two miles peters out along an old water ditch in the woods.

5. Smuggler/Hunter Creek Loop

Round Trip: (from town) 7.5 miles, 1–2 hours
Elevation Gain: 1,200'
Difficulty: Intermediate/Advanced, Strenuous
Map: p. 17

Notes: The Smuggler/Hunter Creek Loop starts with a good stiff climb up the Smuggle Mountain Road, finishes with a fast and thrilling trip down Red Mountain and takes in some jeep road and single track in the middle to make it the finest short route near Aspen.

Access: (See Route #2)

Route: Ascend Smuggler Mountain Road to the platform turnoff 1.6 miles up Smuggler Mountain, turn left onto another dirt road which climbs moderately for a third of a mile to the Iowa Mine dump. After crossing the top of the dump, the road plunges left into a winding, rolling half-mile descent to the Hunter Creek Valley. At the valley floor the road turns sharply right and climbs gently through the woods and meadows to

the Reservoir Bridge, 1 ½ miles further on. Standard procedure is to turn left just before the creek onto the single track that takes you back to the start of the Hunter Creek Trail on Red Mountain and the road into town. You can also cross the creek over Reservoir Bridge and follow the easier, more open Hunter Valley Trail left for a mile back to the Tenth Mountain Bridge on the left, crossing it to rejoin the Hunter Creek Trail to the right for the final mile back to pavement and the downhill into town.

A quiet fall day in Hunter Creek.

6. Four Corners

Round Trip: (from Mill Street Bridge in Aspen) 12.5 miles, 2–4 hours
Elevation Gain: 2,000'
Difficulty: Intermediate, Moderate
Map: p. 17

Notes: The climb to Four Corners was forever altered in the fall of 1995—the main segment was regraded from 4-wheel drive to driveway standard to serve a developable mining claim at the bottom of Van Horn Park. When or if a house is built there remains to be seen—simply regrading the road has served to suburbanize an important chunk of the Aspen backcountry. What was a somewhat challenging climb is now a 2-mile spin. Still, such temporary features as graded roads and Lincoln Log mansions are hardly a match for the mountains—as you climb up out of Hunter Creek the views up into the Williams Mountains and back over Aspen into the Elk Mountains keep expanding, until the road finally crests out of the valley and enters the ridge-top world of wide, open parks and quiet spruce/fir forest. From the Four Corners road crossing on top of the ridge, a half dozen return routes and longer loop rides branch out in all directions, most notably the Sunnyside Trail (see Route #7) and Lenado Loop (see Route #9).

Access: (See Route #4)

Route: From the trailhead by the split-rail fence by Hunter Creek Road, it's about ¼ mile of level riding to the Benedict Bridge over Hunter Creek. The route continues up an old roadbed, somewhat steeply at first, and levels off in the open valley. Shortly after the National Forest sign at the edge of the valley a left fork crosses Hunter Creek (about 1 mile above Benedict Bridge). Take this fork over the Tenth Mountain Bridge. A tenth of a mile after the bridge, turn left onto a 4-wheel drive road near a tumble-down barn and some old cabins. The road goes back down the creek a short distance, then bears right up and across an old pasture. As you approach a fence line, turn right onto the newly graded road that goes up the hill to the right and begins working its way back up the side of the Hunter Creek Valley and in and out of ephemeral creek drainages. Just past the second creek gully, 2.3 miles above the Tenth Mountain Bridge, a single track crosses the road on a nearly direct line down the side of the ridge. The trail to the right is known as "The Plunge"—a steep, rocky expert descent route back to the Hunter Creek Valley. To the left is the Sunnyside hiking trail. On a bike it's a steady, strenuous climb or a smooth, fast alternate descent from Four Corners.

The Sunnyside bike route begins not here, but at Four Corners.

A quarter mile past the trail crossing, the road pitches up and over the top of the glacier-scoured valley wall. Here the road forks; the left fork climbs moderately and enjoyably for another mile through the forest to Four Corners and on to Lenado (see Route #9), the right fork leads across a marshy meadow and then up to Van Horn Park (see Route #8).

Alternate Descents: Besides returning the way you came, from Four Corners, you can go to either the left or the right to return by a slightly different route. If you go left, follow the road along the crest of the ridge for .6 miles to a small sign that says "Sunnyside Trail." This marks the upper end of the hiking trail you passed on the way up. Follow it down to the road, where you can turn right to retrace your ascent route, or cross the road and take The Plunge.

The right fork at Four Corners takes you along the ridge for a short distance, then starts dropping down through the woods to the right and into the northern arm of Van Horn Park (see Route #8). When the trail meets the road, go right for .8 mile to rejoin the ascent route.

7. Sunnyside Trail

Round Trip: (from Mill Street Bridge in Aspen) 15 miles, 3–5 hours
Elevation Gain: 2,500'
Difficulty: Expert, Strenuous
Map: p. 17

Notes: The Sunnyside Trail is the premier ride in the upper valley—great sidehill and downhill single-tracking, incredible views, and some of the best fall colors around. From Four Corners, the Sunnyside Trail traverses through the aspen groves on the south face of Red Mountain, with frequent lookouts over the whole Roaring Fork Valley and the Maroon Bells, then descends a long spur through the Starwood subdivision to McLain Flats Road just above the Rio Grande Trail. The pricey Red Mountain and Starwood estates, marketed for their panoramic views, lie 1,500' below the Sunnyside, back in suburbia. The Sunnyside isn't treacherously difficult, neither is it for the faint of heart.

Access: (See Route #4). Follow Route #6 to Four Corners.

Route: At Four Corners, turn left onto a dirt road, which climbs gently along the crest of the ridge through a quiet lodgepole forest. At .6 miles, a small "Sunnyside Trail" sign marks a single track that drops down off the ridge to the left. Do not take this trail! It's the Sunnyside hiking route and will take you back to the last creek crossing before the Van Horn Park fork—a pleasant enough descent, but not where you want to go.

Stay on the road for another .6 miles and fork left onto an abandoned jeep road that begins to drop off the ridge. After ¼ mile it bears right up a short, steep hill and onto an aspen-covered bench on the south shoulder of Red Mountain. The bench soon peters out and the trail sidehills across the south face for over a mile—exhilarating and not too tricky, but a little overwhelming if you're not used to sidehill riding. Eventually you reach the saddle at the west end of the mountain, where a side route, the Shadyside Trail, forks back to the right and contours around the north side of the mountain through a dark fir forest to rejoin the dirt road just west of the Sunnyside turnoff. That road itself deadends at the microwave relays on the summit of Red Mountain. Between the Sunnyside, Shadyside, Van Horn Park, and the various descents from Four Corners, it's possible to spend several hours looping around up here before returning to civilization.

On the west side of the saddle, the Sunnyside Trail climbs a short steep pitch to the top of a knoll, from which it drops 3 miles and 2,000' back to the Roaring Fork River. The first mile is a pleasant, winding descent through fir and aspen, then the trail turns out of the forest into short scrub oak, opening up views of Aspen, Starwood, and the airport. The descent through the short scrub is rocky and tricky in spots; as the oak gets taller around you the trail becomes a smooth, winding track again.

Riding through golden aspen on the Sunnyside Trail.

Just as you're getting into the rhythm of it, the trail dumps you onto the driveway of a space age mansion. Cross the driveway and walk down a couple of steps, work your way through a couple of tight switchbacks, and enjoy the twists and turns and drop-offs the rest of the way to McLain Flats Road. Turn left on the pavement, shoot down the hill and take a left onto the Rio Grande Trail just before the Slaughterhouse Bridge to get back downtown. This could be the trickiest part of the ride—dodging neophyte bikers, joggers, walkers, skaters, dogs, and children—so lay back and enjoy a well-earned warm-down.

8. Van Horn Park

Round Trip: (from Mill Street Bridge in Aspen) 12.5 miles, 2–4 hours
Elevation Gain: 2,000'
Difficulty: Advanced, Strenuous
Map: p. 17

Notes: Van Horn Park is a classic mountain park—a large natural meadow high in the subalpine forest, bordered by aspen groves and looking out across the Elk Mountains. This is a destination ride with no loop connections, essentially an alternate finish to the Four Corners route with a couple of spurs and a single track variation for the exploratory-minded.

Access: (See Route #4). Follow Route #6 to the road fork ¼ mile past the Sunnyside/Hunter Valley Trail intersection.

Route: Take the right fork onto a dirt road across a long, marshy meadow. At the end of the meadow, the road bears left and up through the woods for .2 miles, then levels out as Van Horn Park opens up before you. The road follows the creek across the level bottom of the park for almost ½ mile, then climbs a long, moderate hill to the top of the park.

From the top of the park you can return the way you came, or take a right fork of the road at the top of the park to get to an advanced single track that loops around to the lower, marshy meadow. Follow the right fork down a draw for a third of a mile; where the road bends left into the woods fork right onto a single track (Forest Service Hunter Creek Trail). The trail sidehills along the Hunter Creek Valley wall—with spectacular views up Hunter Creek to the Williams Mountains—then crosses back over a ridge and winds down through the woods to rejoin the Van Horn Park Road which you follow back to the valley floor. This single track loop can be ridden in the other direction as well.

9. Lenado Loop

Round Trip: (Aspen–Lenado–Woody Creek–Aspen) 24 miles, 2–4 hours.
Elevation Gain: 2,700′
Difficulty: Advanced, Strenuous
Map: pp. 14, 17

Notes: A fine mixed ride, the Lenado Loop combines Four Corners, Lenado Road, and the Rio Grande Trail into a long but not overly taxing ride. The riding varies from paved road to gravel and 4-wheel drive roads to fast single-tracking. The usual way to do the loop is to ride from Aspen up to Four Corners, down through Lenado to Woody Creek, with a stop at the Woody Creek Tavern (where real bikers are preferred, but cyclists are tolerated, especially if they're a little muddy) before slogging back up the Rio Grande Trail to town. But the loop rides just as well the other way, particularly the old wagon road from Lenado up to Four Corners which climbs steadily and moderately for 2 full miles. The trick is finding the poorly marked trailhead in Lenado; it's better to do the loop the usual way the first time out.

Access: (See Route #4). Follow Route #6 to Four Corners.

Route: Continue straight on through the Four Corners road crossing and down a gentle hill. The road ends at a hunting camp on the right; bear left into the woods on a single track which then turns sharply right at the rim of the Woody Creek valley wall. Here you can see traces of the wagon road the miners cut into the side of the canyon; the trail sits on a narrow shelf which is mostly wide enough for comfort but seems to narrow down at all the tricky spots. After the first mile and a couple of interesting gully crossings, the sideslope eases off and the trail switches back and forth through the forest, then crosses some old mine dumps just before reaching the graded gravel road in Lenado. Lenado is a mining camp turned lumber camp turned deliberately downscale Aspen suburb, a half-mile stretch of road with old cabins in varied states of restoration on either side.

Turn left onto the road (Lenado Road) and follow it for 8 miles of gentle downhill to Woody Creek; the last 3 miles of the road are paved as it passes through open ranchland on the valley bottom and the benches on either side. At the end of the road make a sharp left onto the Woody Creek Road—the Tavern is only a quarter of a mile ahead. To get back to town, keep going on the Woody Creek Road for another mile to the bridge across the Roaring Fork. Cross the 3-way intersection into Jaffee Park, a large parking area for fishermen and boaters, and ride through to the far end. Take the rough single track that leads up a gully to the left (the attractive trail along the river deadends about a mile upstream). At the top of the gully bear right onto the Rio Grande Railroad right-of-way, which will take you the rest of the way into Aspen. Four miles further upstream the dirt trail becomes a paved bike path at the Slaughterhouse Bridge, just 2 miles from the end of the ride.

A fine June day—and a gully full of snow on the Lenado Loop.

10. Summer Road

Round Trip: 12 miles, 2–3 hours

Elevation Gain: 3,300′

Difficulty: Advanced, Very Strenuous

Map: p. 26

Notes: This ride up the face of Aspen Mountain is for the hard core only; most of the road is unremittingly steep, dusty, and hot. That said, it's a worthy test piece and doing even the first couple of miles is a good training workout. Because the road switches back and forth across the ski runs, the ambiance is light industrial and the views aren't worth much until you get to the top, which is more easily and scenically reached via the Midnight Mine Road (see Route #11) or Little Annie Road (see Route #12) on the back side of the mountain.

Access: From the Little Nell Hotel on Durant Street, go east one block to Original Street, then right for a block to the end of Original at Ute Avenue. Keep going straight up a driveway which curves right and climbs steeply to a gate at the edge of the Little Nell ski run. Go through the gate and you're on your way.

Route: The road switches back and forth a few times on Little Nell (ski slope), then traverses all the way across to the west side of the ski area where the climbing begins in earnest. When you encounter several spur roads on the lower part of the mountain, keep right and you'll be all right. After passing the snowmaking barn the road switches back up a long, steep cut; two more switchbacks bring you up to the bottom of Ruthie's Run and Ruthie's Restaurant (a good turnaround point for a shortened ride). Another switchback and a pull to the right gets you to the top of Aztec and a very brief respite. One more steep corner, however, and the pitch eases off as the road traverses along the west side of Spar Gulch—there's even a little dip and some level riding as you near Bonnie's Restaurant. At Bonnie's drop down to the left, cross Spar Gulch and climb a ferocious little pitch up to the Bell Mountain saddle. Take heart—only a mile to go, and after the next little pitch it's practically a cruise.

For the return trip, descend the way you came up (a real brake-burner), or go around the gondola building and bear right onto the Midnight Mine Road (see Route #11) which will take you down to the Castle Creek Road three miles south of town.

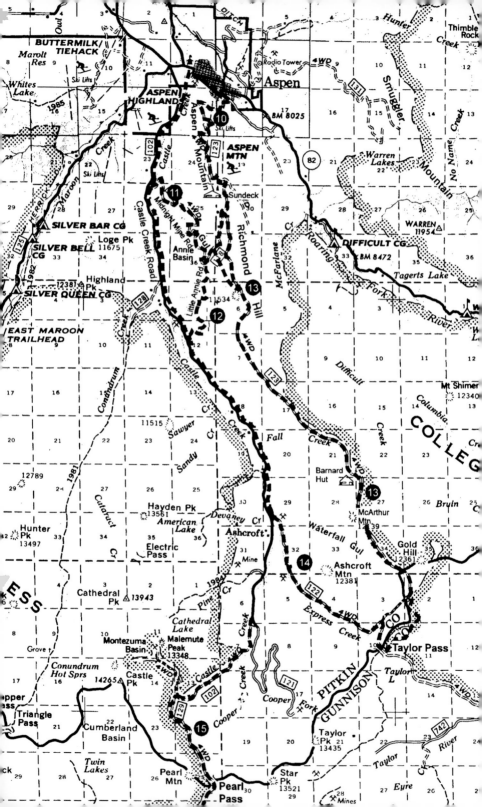

11. Midnight Mine Road

Round Trip: 18 miles, 3–5 hours
Elevation Gain: 3,300' (high point: 11,212')
Difficulty: Intermediate, Strenuous
Map: p. 26

Notes: The most enjoyable ride up Aspen Mountain, the Midnight Mine Road climbs steadily up the east side of Castle Creek, wanders through dark timber in Queen's Gulch, and then emerges near the top of the Little Annie Basin for spectacular views up Conundrum and Castle creeks. Here the Midnight Mine Road joins the Little Annie Road, after which an easy traverse and short climb back to the north takes you to the Sundeck on top of Aspen Mountain. Of the three roads on Aspen Mountain, Midnight Mine is the smoothest going down, and it combines well with either the Summer Road (Route #10) or Little Annie Road (Route #12) for loop rides.

Access: From downtown Aspen, ride west on Hopkins Avenue (one block south of, and parallel to, Main Street). Where Hopkins ends at 7th Street, follow the Bike Route sign to the left around a curve, then turn right onto the bike path. Cross the bridge over Castle Creek, then bear left around the old Marolt Barn (now a Historical Society museum), through the Music School/employee housing, and up a short hill to Castle Creek Road. Turn left and ride 2 ½ gently climbing miles up Castle Creek to the Midnight Mine Road, which forks left and down to the creek.

Route: After crossing the creek, the Midnight Mine Road bears left and climbs diagonally up the hill through the aspen trees. The numerous private drives off this part of the road are all well posted—if not gated as well. After ¼ mile the road turns sharply to the right and begins a long, moderate climb out of Castle Creek and into Queens Gulch, broken by a couple of steep switchbacks. About halfway up the road (2.4 miles, 1,500') is the Midnight Mine itself, with a ruined mill on the left and a prominent tailings dump on the right. The road climbs steeply over the top of the tailings and begins working its way up the other side of the gulch. The pitch is more varied here, giving you a few breaks and changes of pace. As you approach the top of the ridge the climb eases off and the forest opens up; another little patch of woods and you're looking across the Little Annie Basin at Hayden Peak rising 4,000' above the glacial valleys on either side.

At this point the road forks; the left goes to the Sundeck on top of Aspen Mountain, a mile to the north and 600' higher up. The right sends you down the Little Annie Road (see Route #12) to Castle Creek Road and 7 miles of fast pavement back to town, a nice clean loop if you don't feel the need to top out and mix with the crowd at the Sundeck.

12. Little Annie Road

Round Trip: (from Aspen) 22 miles, 4–6 hours/
(from Castle Creek Road) 9 miles, 2–4 hours
Elevation Gain: 3,300'/2,300'
Difficulty: Intermediate, Strenuous
Map: p. 26

Notes: The easiest of the three roads up Aspen Mountain, the Little Annie Road starts a thousand feet above the main valley floor and is shorter and generally less steep than either the Summer or Midnight Mine Roads. Because much of it is on south-facing slopes, it's much more open than the Midnight Mine Road, giving you frequent and expanding views of Highlands Peak, Hayden Peak, and the long jagged ridges flanking the Conundrum and Castle Creek valleys. Little Annie Road is also the first to open in the spring; the lower part is kept open by the people who live along it, and the Aspen Skiing Company plows the upper part in late April to get access to the top of Aspen Mountain. If you do ride up before the snow has melted out (in mid to late June), go early in the morning to avoid the afternoon mudbath. And because the real mountain biking starts 7 miles out of town, many people drive up Castle Creek Road and park at the turnoff—which lowers the work load considerably.

Access: By car, go west out of Aspen on Main Street, across the Castle Creek Bridge, and turn left at the stoplight at Maroon Creek Road. Immediately turn left again onto Castle Creek Road and drive almost 7 miles to where the Little Annie Road doubles back to the left. A road sign is on the left and a pull-off for parking on the right. If you're driving upvalley toward Aspen look for the stone church on your right just before you enter Aspen; turn right onto Maroon Creek Road at the light directly below the church and immediately left onto Castle Creek Road.

By bike, you can avoid traffic and save a little distance from Aspen by going west on Hopkins Street (parallel to Main Street and one block south) to its end, turn left onto 7th Street, and right onto the bike path. Cross the bridge, loop around the right side of the old barn and up through the Marolt housing complex to Castle Creek Road. Turn left and ascend 6.5 easy/moderate miles (1,000' gain) to the Little Annie turnoff.

Route: The first mile or so of Little Annie Road climbs up through a hillside subdivision, then cuts eastward into the bottom of Hurricane Gulch. Coming out of the gulch, the road climbs steeply up a rocky, open hillside and then back through aspen trees into a deep spruce/fir stand. A side road bears left past some cabins; keep climbing through the dark woods and out into the Little Annie Basin, a wide open natural park. The road switchbacks up through the park, with wider views at every turn, to meet the Midnight Mine Road on top of the westward-trending ridge that forms the north side of the basin. Bear right here for another, easier mile to the top of Aspen Mountain. Left will take you back down the Midnight Mine Road to Castle Creek Road and Aspen.

13. Richmond Hill Road

Round Trip: (loop: Little Annie, Richmond Hill, Taylor Pass, Castle Creek roads) 24 miles, 6–8 hours.
Elevation Gain: 3,600' (high point 12,300')
Difficulty: Intermediate, Strenuous
Map: p. 26

Notes: Richmond Hill is the long ridge that stretches south from Aspen Mountain to Gold Hill just above Taylor Pass. To the east are views of the high peaks along the Continental Divide; to the west views of most of the Elk Mountains. While riding the ridge itself is relatively easy, getting there requires a 2,500' climb up from Castle Creek, and only once does the Richmond Hill Road dip below 11,000'. This sustained high altitude is both the joy and the pain of the route. The air is very thin, and if you're not well acclimated you may well experience a bit of altitude sickness; the ridgetop line also leaves you exposed to every passing thunderstorm. Richmond Hill is best done during stable weather, with an early start to further reduce the probability of encountering afternoon storms.

Access: (See Route #12). Follow the Little Annie Road to the Midnight Mine Road.

Route: From the junction of the Little Annie and Midnight Mine roads, continue on toward the Sundeck for ¼ mile, then turn right onto a road that slabs up across the steep, open Little Annie face (fabulous powder skiing in the winter) to join the Richmond Hill Road at its top. You can also ride all the way to the Sundeck and turn sharply back to the right just behind the gondola building to pick up the road at its start.

From the top of the Little Annie face, the main road bears left behind a large knoll; a side road goes up over the knoll (the top of Hurricane

Beating out a summer storm on Richmond Ridge.

Gulch) and rejoins the main road on the other side. At the south end of the knoll the main road regains the ridge line which it follows for 2 miles through sparse woods broken by wide meadows with even wider views. The road then drops 400' down through heavy timber to cross the south end of a long, boggy meadow and immediately starts a steep climb up a fire-thinned hillside to regain the lost altitude. Once there it wanders for a mile through small, timbered knolls and behind the Barnard ski touring hut and around another open, boggy meadow. On the far side of this meadow the road climbs a long gradual draw up past McArthur Mountain and out onto the alpine tundra. This is the most spectacular part of the ride with no trees to block your views or the feeling of being on top of the world.

After crossing the saddle between McArthur Mountain and Gold Hill, the road climbs a wearying 500' up to the Gold Hill ridge line. Here the Richmond Hill Road enters a maze of jeep roads and trails; keep heading straight south toward the next hill with your road switchbacking up it. From the top of this second hill the descent begins: ½ mile southwest to

Taylor Pass just above round Taylor Lake, then right onto the Taylor Pass Road (see Route #14), and 5.5 miles down to Ashcroft and Castle Creek Road. Four miles to the right down Castle Creek is the Little Annie turnoff where your epic began.

Note: At the saddle between the last two hills on the Richmond Hill Road, an abandoned jeep road turns off to the right and follows the upper end of Express Creek down to join the Taylor Pass Road .7 miles below the top. It's a loose, cobbly, bouldery, expert descent for those who like that sort of thing, but it saves you a mile of climbing and descending that last hill to the pass.

14. Taylor Pass (Express Creek Road)

Round Trip: (from Ashcroft) 11 miles, 2–4 hours
Elevation Gain: 2,530'
Difficulty: Advanced, Strenuous
Map: p. 26

Notes: A truly enjoyable hill climb, challenging without being an endless grind, this route combines short, steep stretches with gentler intervals that give you time to recover and enjoy the scenery of a lovely alpine valley. The last grunt to the top of the pass rewards you with a panoramic view of the heavily forested Taylor River Valley and western slopes of the Collegiate Range. At 11,928' Taylor Pass sits just above the tree line, and even on a hot summer day holds the slightly giddy chill of the wide-open alpine tundra. Taylor Pass is popular with 4-wheelers and dirt bikers as well as mountain bikers, so expect a bit of traffic, especially on weekends and holidays. Due to the altitude, Taylor Pass is ridable in mid-June at the earliest. Check with a bike shop or the Forest Service for road conditions.

Access: From the Maroon Creek intersection just west of Aspen, go south on Castle Creek Road (an immediate left turn after turning onto Maroon Creek Road from Highway 82) 10.5 miles, ½ mile shy of the ghost town of Ashcroft. The Taylor Pass Road (officially known as Express Creek Road) angles off to the left toward the creek. A half-dozen parking spaces are located down by the creek; if these are full you can go just up Castle Creek Road to the large public lot across from the Toklat Lodge.

Route: From the bridge across Castle Creek, the road starts climbing fairly steeply up the side of the valley to a sometimes tricky stream crossing. After the crossing, the pitch eases off to a smooth, rolling ascent through the aspen forest. As the road rounds into the Express Creek valley it crosses several avalanche paths coming down from Ashcroft Mountain on the left; you may see broken trees and other debris and possibly an out-of-place patch of snow. The first mile along Express Creek is a gentle climb through more aspen, then the terrain gets rockier and the road takes two steep, loose steps up to the sparsely wooded subalpine region. After an open, mile-long flat, the valley turns sharply left and the road goes up another steep pitch. By now you should be feeling the altitude; after one last respite the road crosses the creek and turns back to the right for the final ¾-mile grunt to the top.

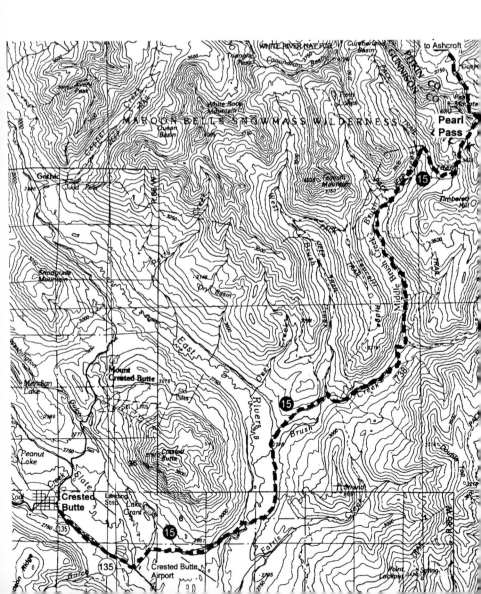

15. Pearl Pass Road to Crested Butte

Round Trip: (from Ashcroft to Pearl Pass) 13 miles, 4–6 hours
One Way: (from Ashcroft to Crested Butte) 25 miles, 5–8 hours
Elevation Gain: 3,000'
Difficulty: Advanced/Expert, Strenuous
Map: pp. 26, 32

Notes: At 12,705' Pearl Pass is the highest pass in the Roaring Fork Valley; as the most direct route between Crested Butte and Aspen it's also the Grande Dame of alpine bike tours. When Fat Tire Bike Week began in Crested Butte in the early eighties, its culmination was the ride across Pearl Pass to the Jerome Bar in Aspen. At that time mountain bikes were virtually unknown in Aspen, and the sight of mud-spattered riders humping down Main Street on knobby-tired clunkers was a real attention getter. Now that's no big deal, but the ride still is. The top of the pass is rarely snow-free for more than a month (August-September) and the roughness of the road and the exposure to the weather are greater than on any other ride in the area. The ride across the tundra below 14,250' Castle Peak and the ensuing summit view from the pass that encompasses the Sawatch Range to the north and the San Juan Mountains to the south across the Gunnison Valley are unparalleled.

Access: From Aspen, go west on Main Street and ½ mile out of town to the Maroon Creek Road intersection. Turn left off Highway 82 and immediately left again onto Castle Creek Road. From here it is 12 ½ miles to the end of the pavement and the beginning of the Pearl Pass/Montezuma Basin Road. Park where the pavement ends and the road forks: the right fork is the road to Pearl Pass.

Route: The road meanders along the level valley floor for ½ mile before making a short, steep climb up to and around a small reservoir on the right. Another ½ mile of easy riding through the woods brings you to a bridge across Castle Creek; past the bridge a nasty little climb through loose rocks and gravel gets you up to the next level of the valley. Here the road climbs pleasantly for 1 ½ miles through dark timber broken by the broad swaths of avalanche paths coming down from Mace Peak on the left. At 11,000' the road crosses the creek again and climbs a couple of steep, rocky switchbacks to another fork in the road: the right fork follows the main valley up to Montezuma Basin, a rocky, 2-mile grunt with spectacular views; the left fork goes to Pearl Pass. The next mile of the Pearl Pass Road past the Tagert and Wilson/Green ski-touring huts and up onto the tundra is steep and loose, and entails more pushing than

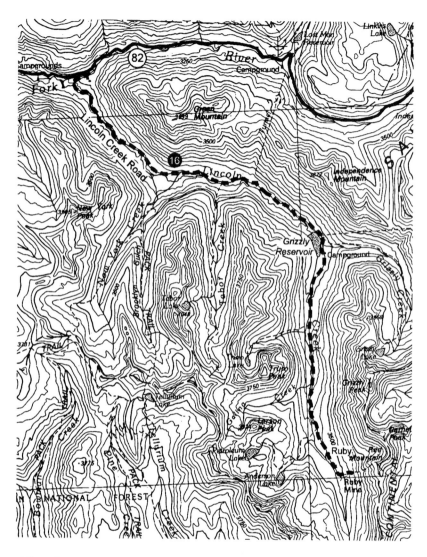

riding. But once on top of the high, spectacularly situated bench below Pearl Mountain, the riding is surprisingly smooth and level until you reach the broad scree field just below the summit of the pass. The road here is full of loose, but well compacted, small rocks, and you should be able to ride most of way to the top.

The other side is another story—the traverse around the south side of Pearl Mountain starts out benignly enough, then the road turns into a pile of cantaloupes for ½ mile. The condition of the road gradually improves as it drops down off the tundra plateau, and once it reaches timber and bends back to the north for the run down to Middle Brush Creek, it's almost a cruise. And the 5-mile run down Middle Brush to the junction with East Brush Creek is a smooth fast one, through long grassy meadows and shady aspen groves—a taste of mountain biking Crested Butte style. After a major ford across the creek, the road runs level across a meadow for a mile, then climbs up around a small canyon and out into the rangeland above the East River, the Butte itself rising up on the other side. A long traversing descent brings you down to the river bottom and the old Brush Creek Cow Camp. Keep heading downstream on the improved road, cross the river and climb up past the airport and the golf course and out to the highway for the final 2-mile grunt into town.

16. Lincoln Creek Road

Round Trip: (from Highway 82 to Grizzly Reservoir) 12 miles, 2–4 hours/
(from Highway 82 to Ruby) 22 miles, 3–6 hours
Elevation Gain: 800'/1,700'
Difficulty: Novice/Intermediate, Moderate
Map: p. 34

Notes: A fine alpine ride without the usual struggle to get there, Lincoln Creek is a good introduction to high country biking. The climbing is moderate and the classic glacial valley is flanked by 12,000' ridges with 13,000' peaks. In addition to the ride there are good hikes up New York, Tabor, Grizzly, and Truro creeks, fishing at the reservoir, and a spectacular swimming hole in the deep river potholes along the way. The drawback is that Lincoln Creek is a very popular all-around playground and you'll find more traffic here than on any of the other backcountry roads. Best to go during the week if you can manage it.

Access: Take Highway 82 ten miles east from Aspen to Lincoln Creek Road (on the right 2 miles past the Weller Lake Campground). You can park at the turnoff; if this is too crowded, drive down the hill to the Lincoln Creek Campground and park in the general parking area there.

Route: From the highway the Lincoln Creek Road drops back down along the Roaring Fork River for several hundred yards; at the bottom of a set of switchbacks the campground road turns off to the right. Keep left; the road follows the level creek bottom for about a mile, then begins a winding, stair-stepping climb up to the potholes and the swimming/sunbathing crowd. It's a fun section to ride—especially on the way down—but stay mindful of the cars, often piloted by green backcountry drivers. Once past the potholes, the climb slackens off to a nearly level cruise the remaining 4 miles to Grizzly Reservoir. Grizzly is part of the major water diversion that collects Western Slope snowmelt and sends it through a system of tunnels under the Continental Divide to eastern Colorado—in this case to the Arkansas River and the Pueblo area.

To continue on toward Ruby, pass around the reservoir on the left. Once past the reservoir the traffic is minimal, the landscape open, and the peaks craggy. It's worth going on a mile or two, if not the full 5 miles to the remains of the mining camp of Ruby among the willows at tree line. The riding is a little more technical and the climbing more sustained, but by no means is it difficult.

A spring-fed stream near Ruby on the Lincoln Creek Road.

Snowmass Village

Snowmass is a veritable rat's nest of ridable roads and trails that run through and around the Village, and all across, up, and down the sprawling ski area. It makes for good riding but rough writing, sorting out and keeping up with the changes as the town and ski area grow and evolve. New trails are being built, old ones re-aligned, and the Aspen Skiing Company is experimenting with summer lift access for mountain bikers. The rides described here are main established routes; for more detailed information on the Village and ski area riding, check with the Snowmass Mall information center and the Aspen Skiing Company.

17. Rim Trail

Round Trip: (from Mall) 10 miles, 1 ½–2 ½ hours
Elevation Gain: 2,000'
Difficulty: Intermediate/Advanced, Strenuous
Map: p. 39

Notes: The Rim Trail is an interesting ride along the crest of the ridge west of Snowmass Village with some excellent winding single track and a few problems: a handful of unridable steep sections along the ridge line. An expert rider can get down them, but shouldn't—there's already a rut down the center of the trail that only increases erosion. The good news is that the town of Snowmass Village is looking for a way to improve these sections; the two ends of the trail are superbly crafted for mountain biking and most of the ridge is fine as is. You can also ride 1 mile up Sinclair Road (on the left, 1 mile down Brush Creek Road from the Snowmass Center) to the midpoint of the Rim Trail and ride just the northern half, which eliminates all of the steep drops.

Access: From the Snowmass Village Mall take the Loop Road west across Brush Creek and up to the intersection with the Divide Road (.4 miles). Turn left onto the Divide Road and immediately right into the Mountain View housing complex. Turn left out of the driveway and right onto the trail—a single track up a berm.

Route: After a tricky little start, the trail moderates into a steady climb that switchbacks up through the grass and brush. A few of the turns are difficult, but most are quite negotiable and the climb gets easier as you approach the ridge line 1.3 miles from the trailhead. At the ridge line (with views back across the village and the ski area, and ahead down into

The Rim Trail grants sweeping views of Snowmass and the peaks beyond.

Snowmass Creek) turn right and make a short climb along a fence line to the height of land—a narrow ridge that drops precipitously on the east side. Luckily there's a hedge of scrub oak between the trail and the edge of the bluff all the way. From this height of land the trail makes its first walk-down plunge, then rolls smoothly along the ridge for a good ½ mile before the second walker. There are a couple more in the next ¾ mile as the trail works its way down to the saddle between Melton Ranch (the subdivision on the right) and Wildcat Ranch (the exclusive zone on the left). A moderate push leads up to a knob capped by a large house, and another steep downhill brings you to a road crossing.

Go straight across the road toward a gate, then right up a hill along the fence. From here on the ride mellows out with a good ½ mile of level riding along the ridge above Horse Ranch, then a gradually steepening climb ending with a push up to the last high point, 1 ¼ miles from the road crossing. The 2-mile descent starts with ¼ mile of slightly gullied old trail, then the bike route forks right and away from the equestrian route onto a new trail that rolls smoothly down through the aspen and scrub to the Horse Ranch subdivision. As you approach the first houses, stay left on the single track at a T-junction to rejoin the equestrian trail for ¼ mile until the single track merges with a double track. Stay left again, the double track becomes graveled and finally ends at a subdivision street. Follow the main Horse Ranch road out to Brush Creek Road. To get back to the Mall (2 ½ miles), ride up Brush Creek Road or along the bike path which parallels it on the east side.

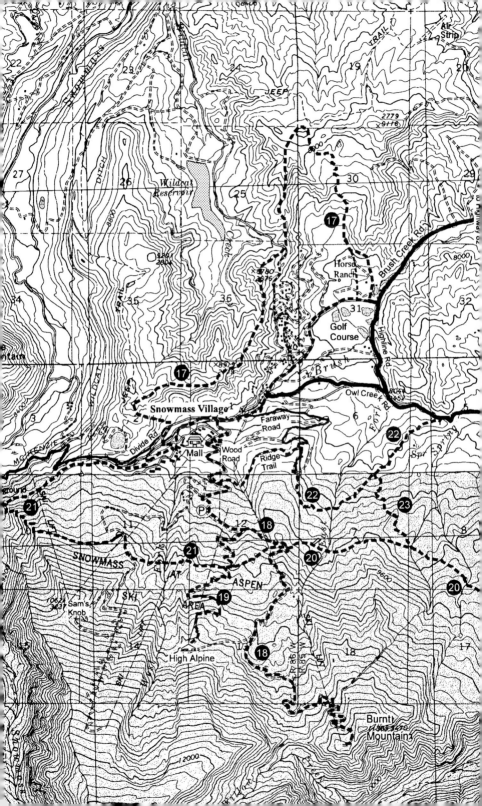

18. Elk Camp Road

Round Trip: (from Wood Road) 10 miles, 2–3 hours
Elevation gain: 2,200'
Difficulty: Intermediate, Strenuous
Map: p. 39

Notes: The Snowmass Ski Area is home to a plethora of service roads. For the serious rider Elk Camp Road is clearly the best—a stiff, but not overly demanding ride through a lovely landscape ending with a world-class view encompassing West Willow Creek and the Maroon Bells.

Access: From Snowmass Village Center head 2 miles up Wood Road to its end. Bear left onto a dirt road and down a short hill to a parking area.

Route: Turn off Wood Road onto Elk Camp Road; continue past the parking area and begin climbing easily across the side of the mountain. After ½ mile (by the intersection with High Alpine Road) the road turns more up the hill and climbs moderately across Funnel Run to the intersection with the Government Trail. Switch back through the woods and cross a flat to the base of the Elk Camp lift, continue past the lift in a southwesterly direction and climb through the woods again to the base of Hanging Valley Wall—a steep, ungroomed powder preserve rimmed by a rock band which skiers must penetrate via a handful of narrow gullies. The road heads south and east again, switchbacking up over sparsely wooded ridges to the top of the ski runs at a lovely timberline saddle.

19. High Alpine Road

Round Trip: (from Wood Road) 6 miles, 1–2 hours
Elevation Gain: 1,300'
Difficulty: Beginner, Strenuous
Map: p. 39

Notes: High Alpine Road is not as spectacular as the Elk Camp Road a mile to the east, but is considerably smoother and easier, with good outlooks across the Brush Creek Valley.

Access: (See Route #18). Follow Elk Camp Road for ½ mile, then turn uphill onto the High Alpine Road.

Route: The road switchbacks up the fall line between the Naked Lady run and the High Alpine quad lift, in and out of the forest until it tops out at the High Alpine Restaurant.

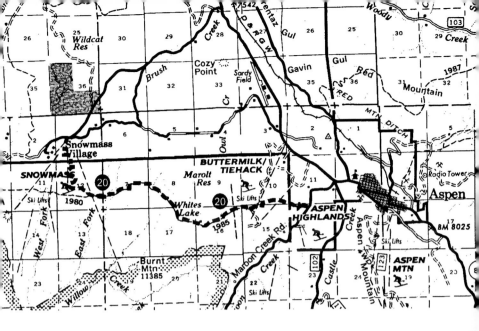

20. Government Trail

One Way: (Snowmass Center to Iselin Park) 11 miles, 2–4 hours
Elevation Gain: 1,500'
Difficulty: Advanced, Moderate
Maps: pp. 39, 41

Notes: The Government Trail is the classic Aspen single track—there are finer trails around, but the Government Trail was readily accessible and memorably challenging, so it was the first to be used and talked up. As a result, the trail is now a bit battered in some sections that weren't built for heavy traffic. But it will still batter you in others, and the poorly designed sections are up for rehabilitation or replacement. The route is a long traverse from the Snowmass Ski Area across the East Brush and Owl Creek drainages and the Buttermilk Ski Area, down to Maroon Creek near the Highlands. The climbing is minimal, but there are a lot of rough, tricky stream crossings; the track varies from silky smooth dirt to the infamous Rock Garden. Neither this route nor Government Trail West (see Route #21) is worth riding in reverse. The Government Trail is closed until the end of June for elk calving; it's muddy and mosquito-infested at that time of year anyway, and is best ridden in late summer or the fall.

Access: From the Snowmass Center Conoco (directly below the ski area and the slopeside condos) cross Brush Creek Road onto Wood Road, which winds its way up the mountainside through condos and vacation homes for 2 steady but moderately pitched miles to a cul-de-sac. Exit left onto a gated ski area road that goes down a short hill (there is a parking lot here), and then traverse upward across the ski runs for 1 mile. At the crest of a ridge, where the road bends south into the trees, is the intersection with the Government Trail. To go east (the route described below) drop down the hill to the left, to go west (Route #21) climb up into the trees on the right. Both directions are marked.

The aspen shed their colors along the Government Trail.

Route: The trail drops steeply down off the ridge, then traverses right across a new ski run to the first stream crossing (the easiest one you'll see). Once across the stream the pattern begins that typifies the first section of the trail—traversing out around the ridges and in to cross the creeks, with brief technical difficulties getting back up out of the water. After about 1 mile of this, the trail gets out on the main ridge of Burnt Mountain for another mile of twisty turning but drier and easier riding. Then it drops down off the ridge and through a pair of wide meadows for a level respite before the short, nasty two-stage climb up into the evergreen forest. Once up this hill the trail levels off for a mile of cruising through the woods with only minor difficulties. Nearing Whites Lake, it makes several bouldery dry creek crossings, then rolls merrily through the meadows and aspen along the south side of a fence for ½ mile.

After a short, fast descent to the north, the trail turns sharply right, across another creek bed and into the rough passage of the Rock Garden. Winning racers carry their bikes through here, and you would do well to do the same unless you welcome the challenge of difficult rock-hopping with the likelihood of an upset. The Rock Garden lasts for one tenth of a mile, and leads into the long, smooth descent across the Buttermilk Ski Area. The ski area is divided into three sections; between the west and center the trail is fast and smooth with only a few tight turns and drops, between the center and east is a set of very steep, tight eroded switchbacks that only an expert should attempt. Once across the eastern (Tiehack) ski runs the trail really deteriorates; getting down to Maroon Creek is difficult enough on foot, let alone on a bike—a slight price to pay for such a rewarding ride. Cross the bridge over Maroon Creek and hike up the other side to Maroon Creek Road, cross the road and pick up the bike path system through the public school campus and into Aspen.

21. Government Trail West

Round Trip: (from Snowmass Center) 9 miles, 1 ½–3 hours
Elevation Gain: 1,200'
Difficulty: Advanced, Moderate
Map: p. 39

Notes: Unbeknownst to many riding the Government Trail from Snowmass to Aspen, a western extension of the Government Trail from the Snowmass Ski Area adds 3 miles of fine single track that rides best as a loop (with parts of it fitting into various other possible loops) starting and ending in Snowmass Village. Government Trail West runs straight across the ski area at about knee level, so while it lacks some of the wildland qualities of the eastern section, it matches it for ridability. However, the midsection, between the High Alpine and Coney Glade lifts, can be more than wild enough—its two unbridged streams are dangerously full with meltwater in May and June, and even into July.

Access: (See Route #20)

Route: Just up the Elk Camp Road from the Government Trail trailhead, turn right into the aspen trees and work your way west, across the aptly named Funnel Run, Adams Avenue, Naked Lady, and briefly onto one switchback of the High Alpine Road. Between the High Alpine and Coney Glade quad lifts, the trail runs mostly through thickly wooded gullies unsuited for ski runs. Then the terrain becomes more civilized; the trail merges with a traversing road/ski run to the old Burlingame double chair. Before reaching the chair, leave the road and go left around the top of it, traversing across the flats at the base of Sam's Knob. After crossing under the parallel Sam's Knob and Campground lifts, the trail switchbacks steeply down a ridge to end at the East Snowmass Ditch Trail. Turn right onto the ditch trail and follow it for 1 mile back to the Divide. Here you can pick up the Nature Trail off the right side of the road for another mile of pleasant riding down the creek to the Mall.

22. Two Creeks Trail

One Way: 2 miles, 30 minutes
Elevation Gain: 600'
Difficulty: Intermediate, Moderate
Map: p. 39

Notes: Not a lot of ride in itself, Two Creeks is a vital link in putting together good loops in the lower mountain/East Village area. It's also in the area undergoing the greatest development (1996–2000), but appears destined to stay while many of the trail links around it get rearranged.

Access: From the lower end of Wood Road in Snowmass Village, take the bike path down along Brush Creek Road to Owl Creek Road. Turn right on Owl Creek Road opposite the fire station and follow it for 1 ¼ miles, past the golf course and the intersection with Highline Road, and up the hill to the Snowmass Village maintenance center and the trailhead. Coming from Aspen, take the Owl Creek bike path to the top of the Glendale Divide, take Owl Creek Road down the hill ¼ mile to the maintenance center.

Route: The trail begins on the south side of Owl Creek Road across from the maintenance center and drops off the edge of the road into a narrow field, where it immediately climbs up through the woods on the other side to an old irrigation ditch. Follow the ditch to the right for ¾ of a mile, then bear left up across the hillside. Shortly the Anaerobic Nightmare trail forks left; keep following the old road for another ½ mile and bear right again at the junction with another single track (presently closed). The trail now traverses northward for ½ mile to the top of Faraway Road, which leads back down to Brush Creek Road between the Snowmass Center and the Owl Creek Road intersection. To get back out to the ski area roads and the Mall, go down Faraway Road ¼ mile to the first right-hand switchback and turn left onto the Ridge Trail which will drop you down onto the Funnel Road halfway between the Elk Camp Road and the bottom of the ski area.

23. Anaerobic Nightmare

One Way: (from Owl Creek Road) 2 miles, ½ hour
Elevation Gain: 800'
Difficulty: Advanced, Strenuous
Map: p. 39

Notes: The name is only a slight exaggeration, and for hardriders coming out Owl Creek Road from Aspen, hell bent on fitting the Government Trail into an evening time slot, it's apt—a single track that climbs 600' in short, steep spurts over the course of a mile. It's a difficult but well-placed connecting trail that fits into an Owl Creek–Nightmare–Government Trail loop originating in Aspen, or a Government–Nightmare (downhill)–Owl Creek loop originating in Snowmass Village.

Access: (See Route #22). Follow Two Creeks Trail for about a mile. Shortly after this trail leaves the ditch line, Nightmare forks left up the hill.

Route: The trail winds up the foot of Burnt Mountain, doing its unlevel best to cope with the geologically unstable, hummocky terrain. You've got to do the same, remembering that it's only 1 mile of hell and you can take a rest in the lovely open park at the top before hitting the Government Trail back to Aspen. Coming down from Snowmass it's no sweat at all—just a rollicking run down the hill.

Woody Creek

Woody Creek leads to Lenado, and Lenado leads to a mountain full of old logging roads, mining roads, and pack trails. This section describes the best and most accessible rides in the area but there are plenty more roads and trails for the skilled adventurer to seek out. Get out your topographic maps (but don't give them total credence, the USGS never gets every little road and trail just right) and survival gear (those situations always take you by surprise) and go have some serious fun. West of Woody Creek the Roaring Fork Valley begins to open up; Snowmass and Capitol Creeks are but an introduction to the back road cruising to be done in the mid-valley area.

24. Lenado Road (Woody Creek Road)

Round Trip: (from Woody Creek Tavern) 16 miles, 1–3 hours
Elevation Gain: 1,200'
Difficulty: Beginner, Easy
Map: p. 47

Notes: Usually ridden as an access/egress route to or from the high country, Lenado Road is also a good ride for a beginning mountain biker or someone just beginning their riding season. In combination with the Rio Grande Trail it makes for a moderately long, easy training ride. The first three miles from Woody Creek are paved, the rest is graded dirt/gravel through a quiet mountain canyon. The "town" of Lenado is a refreshingly downscale collection of old and new cabins that was originally an offshoot of Aspen's mining boom.

Access: Ride the Rio Grande Trail (see Route #1) from Aspen to the Woody Creek Tavern (8 miles), or drive 6 miles west from Aspen on Highway 82 to the Woody Creek turnoff. Drop down the hill, cross the river and immediately turn left; the tavern is another mile down the River Road. From the Tavern, continue ¼ mile downriver, then double back to the right onto the Lenado Road (signed as the Woody Creek Road).

Route: The first half of the Lenado Road winds through open ranch country, some of the ranches for real, others haunted by the rich and notorious. Shortly after the road turns to dirt, the valley narrows into a wooded canyon which doesn't open up until you reach the mining camp (Lenado). Near the far end of town is a rough sign in the grass on the right reading "Bike Trail to Aspen." This is Trail 1989 (see Route #9), a

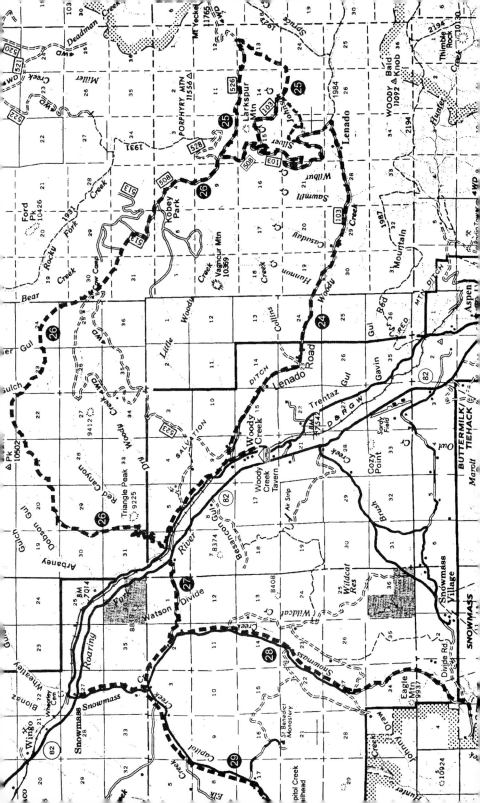

fine climb and descent across the Red Mountain ridge for advanced riders. Around the bend past town, the road crosses Woody Creek and begins climbing to Larkspur Mountain (see Route #25) and Kobey Park (see Route #26). At the bridge is the beginning of the Woody Creek Trail (Trail 1984), a pleasant, infrequently used wilderness hike.

25. Larkspur Mountain

Round Trip: (from Woody Creek Tavern) 36 miles, 4–6 hours
Elevation Gain: 3,900'
Difficulty: Intermediate, Moderate
Map: p. 47

Notes: The mountains to the north and west of Aspen are gentler than the high peaks to the south and east and, when all is said and done, this makes for more enjoyable riding. You go further, see more country, and get the panoramic views that put the high peaks in their regional perspective. Larkspur is the most prominent of the wooded peaks which you can see on the northern horizon from Aspen's ski slopes; the notable feature is a series of wide, grassy slopes on its southern face. The route (which crosses that southern face of Larkspur) is almost entirely on Forest Service logging roads, which are well maintained and offer some great views in all directions; this is a good place to start getting a sense of the larger country between the Roaring Fork and Eagle River valleys.

Access: (See Route #24). At the eastern end of the Lenado settlement, the road goes over a slight ridge and winds its way down to a bridge across the Woody Creek; once across the creek you're on your way up Larkspur Mountain. You can ride from Woody Creek (or even Aspen), or you can park at the Woody Creek trailhead by the bridge and shorten the total distance to 20 miles.

Route: The road climbs steadily, but not too steeply, for 5 miles. The first mile slabs up the east side of Silver Creek, then the road works its way around the southern end of the ridge between Silver and Wilbur creeks and begins switchbacking up toward the crest of the ridge. After about 3 miles it gains the ridge line and follows it to the base of Larkspur. Here the road divides; Forest Road 103 forks right and traverses eastward across Larkspur Mountain above Silver Creek, Forest Road 508 continues climbing on the Wilbur Creek side toward Kobey Park to the northwest.

The junction of Road 103 and Road 508 is one end of the loop around Larkspur Mountain, which can be ridden either way, or out and back on

High above the valley on Larkspur Mountain.

either side. The eastern side, which leads out to the Tenth Mountain Trail's Margy's Hut, is the more interesting and scenic; the final climb is a little more challenging and descending it, conversely, a little more exciting.

For the sake of that descent (and the easier ascent) we'll take the loop clockwise. From the junction, Road 508 continues climbing across the open western face of Larkspur for nearly a mile, then crests out onto the relatively level ridgetop and makes an almost straight run north for ½ mile to the junction with Forest Road 526. Turn right onto Road 526 to complete the Larkspur loop. (Road 508 goes on to Kobey Park and the

Arbaney-Kittle Trail; see Route #26.) Road 526 traverses the steep northern face of Larkspur for ¾ mile, then crosses over a low saddle on a spur ridge. A logging road takes off to the left here, keep right and continue traversing the north side of the ridge above Rocky Fork Creek for another 2 miles. Across the creek is Porphyry Mountain and beyond it more of the densely wooded ridges along the Frying Pan River. To the northwest is the long, flat ridge of Red Table Mountain (see Route #47) and to the northeast the rocky peaks of the Sawatch Range.

The return leg of the loop is easy to miss—a jeep road on the right marked with the blue diamond of the Tenth Mountain Trail. If you do miss it, you will almost immediately come to the turnoff to Margy's Hut on the right; turn back to find the jeep road. The jeep road crosses a slight saddle, then begins its winding, rolling descent back to the graded surface of Road 103. From this perspective, you get clear views across to the Williams Mountains that lie between you and Independence Pass. After Road 103 crosses a ridge point and heads north again, look for an old road with the blue diamonds dropping down to your left. This Johnson/Silver Creek Trail is an exciting (advanced) short cut that will take you down to the first switchback on Road 103 where it crosses Silver Creek a mile above the bridge. If you elect to stay on Road 103, the road traverses around the Silver Creek drainage for another 2 miles to the junction with Road 508 where you began the loop. Go left to continue back down to Lenado.

26. Arbaney-Kittle Trail to Triangle Peak

Round Trip: (from Woody Creek) 28 miles, 5–8 hours
Elevation Gain: 4,600'
Difficulty: Advanced, Very Strenuous
Map: p. 47

Notes: The Arbaney-Kittle Trail has a well-earned reputation as a gonzo route—a lot of hard riding with plenty of opportunities to get off track. The route described here takes in the best and eliminates the worst of the riding, as well as the principal route-finding problem. What remains is the core of the ride—7 miles of superb single-tracking along the ridge between the Roaring Fork and Frying Pan rivers—plus a long workout of a climb to start it, and a long, rough descent to finish you off at the end. The starting climb can be eliminated with a car shuttle up to Kobey Park.

Access: (See Routes #24, #25). At the junction of Forest Road 508 and Forest Road 526 keep going straight on Road 508 toward Kobey Park. If you are doing a shuttle, the best parking spot is ½ mile before the junction, where Road 508 reaches the top of the ridge.

Route: From the junction with Road 526, Road 508 bends left and skirts the western edge of the Rocky Fork Creek drainage for about a mile, then crosses back to the Woody Creek side. Two miles from the start bear right onto Forest Road 513 in the middle of an old clearcut. One

Grunting up one of the many little climbs on the Arbaney-Kittle Trail.

mile further on, during a long gradual descent, the road makes a hairpin turn to the right. Three quarters of a mile after this turn, and 50 yards past a bend to the left, a faint single track forks left into the woods, marked by a rock cairn on the opposite (right) side of the road. This is the easily missed start of the single track; if you follow the road out into a meadow you've gone too far.

The track itself soon leaves the woods and enters the meadow, where it bends left to follow the gentle slope of the drainage. It continues faint until the slope steepens and it becomes rocky and technical for ¼ mile. After crossing a stream it becomes smoother, passes through a meadow with a view of the ridge ahead, and a mile from the crossing merges with a jeep road. Keep right past a cabin and a wetland on the left, climb over a knoll through a gate and drop down to a Forest Service cabin on the left. Past the cabin the trail makes a steep climb straight up the hill to a fork—keep right along the ridge. One-half mile further on is an overlook on the right with views out over Rocky Fork Creek and the Frying Pan Valley. The trail continues left across the south face of the ridge for 1 ½ miles through the aspen forest until breaking out into the open for views of Triangle Peak below and Capitol Peak and Mount Sopris across the valley. Another mile of traversing and climbing brings you to a delightful 1 ½-mile descent through the spruce forest and out into a level meadow.

Cross the meadow on the road and bear right back into the woods, climb a short hill and head south into the long (5 ½-mile) descent. The first ¾ mile runs smoothly down a broad ridgetop, then the ridge steepens and narrows as the road drops down to a stream gully which it follows for another mile, then leaves the drainage to traverse the ridge leading out to Triangle Peak. The road climbs up on the west side of the peak, then begins the long, rocky brake-burning final descent to the Lower River Road. From here the Tavern is a mere 2 ½ miles to the left up Lower/Upper River Road.

27. Watson Divide Road

One Way: 2 miles, 20–30 minutes
Elevation Gain: 450'
Difficulty: Beginner, Moderate
Map: p. 47

Notes: Watson Divide offers beautiful views of the Snowmass/Capitol Creek Valley and Mount Sopris; it is not, however, a "destination" ride. Rather, Watson Divide Road a handy connecting road for getting up and down valley and for access to several back roads. That just happens to have a few rewards of its own.

Access: (from Woody Creek) Follow the Upper River Road downvalley for 2 ½ miles to where the Lower River Road forks right; stay left and drop down the hill to the bridge across the Roaring Fork and up the riverbank on the other side to Highway 82. Go right along Highway 82 for 200 yards and cross over to Watson Divide Road, a gravel road that T's off of Highway 82 on the south side.

(from Snowmass Creek Road) [from the north] Three miles upstream from the Snowmass General Store on Highway 82 (1 ¼ miles after making a left turn at the T-intersection with Capitol Creek Road), Watson Divide Road drops down to a bridge across the creek on the left. [from the south] Coming down Snowmass Creek from the Divide above Snowmass Village (See Route #28) look for the deeply cut switchbacks on your right; the Watson Divide intersection is 3 ½ miles below the transition from gravel to pavement.

Route: From the Woody Creek end, Watson Divide Road climbs gradually up through lush irrigated hayfields for a mile to a short, steep pitch to the top of the divide and a panoramic view across the wide valley to Mount Sopris and the glacier-scalloped Elk Mountain Ridge. After a short, straight run, the road switchbacks steeply down to Snowmass Creek and the road on the other side. From this point there are four options: turn left up Snowmass Creek Road (see Route #28) with the possibility of going all the way up to Snowmass Village; turn right and go down Snowmass Creek to Highway 82, across it and back up the Lower River Road; turn left ¾ mile down Snowmass Creek Road and head up Capitol Creek Road (see Route #29); lastly, start up Capitol Creek and after ½ mile turn right onto East Sopris Creek Road (see Route #36) to Basalt and Carbondale. This last option is probably the most popular—and natural—reason to be going over Watson Divide.

28. Snowmass Creek Road

Round Trip: (from Snowmass General Store) 23 miles, 2–3 hours
Elevation Gain: 1,400'
Difficulty: Beginner, Easy
Map: p. 47

Notes: Snowmass Creek Road and Capitol Creek Road (see #29) are relatively quiet county roads through a pair of expansive, ranch-dominated valleys west of Snowmass Village. The lower, more developed portions of the roads are paved while the upper, more scenic ends are still gravel and dirt. Snowmass Creek Road, which ends at a wilderness trailhead on the valley floor near the creek, is the easier of the two rides.

Access: The Snowmass General Store is on Highway 82, 4 miles east of Basalt and 15 miles west of Aspen. Public parking is along the fence on the upvalley side of the gas station; you can also get there using the RFTA bus system. Long distance riders can use the Rio Grande Trail (Route #1), Upper River Road, and Watson Divide Road (Route #27—a shortcut that bypasses the General Store) to get to Snowmass Creek Road from Aspen. From Basalt take the Basalt Bike Path (Route #35) which goes from Elk Run up along the north side of Highway 82 and the Roaring Fork to join the Lower River Road just across the river from the General Store. From Snowmass Village, ride 1 mile up the Divide Road to the Divide, where the road turns to dirt and descends for 1 ½ miles (moderate) through the Campground ski runs to the upper end of Snowmass Creek Road. Turn right and cross the bridge for a pleasant cruise along Snowmass Creek down to Highway 82.

Route: The Snowmass Creek Road begins at the General Store and heads south to a T-intersection 1 ¾ miles up the creek. This first section has a number of blind curves and usually has a steady flow of traffic—definitely ride single file and be prepared to stay out of the way of large trucks. Once past the intersection the traffic level is lower, though people do tend to drive the road in a hurry. So while you're not likely to see a car more than once in five minutes, please don't get blasé. Go left at the T-intersection to stay on Snowmass Creek Road (Capitol Creek Road is to the right). From the T-intersection, the road runs for a couple of miles across the level flood plain, then begins twisting and gently climbing along the western edge of the valley bottom. The lower part of the valley is dominated by dense scrub oak; as you slowly climb higher the now gravel road winds through groves of aspen and the valley walls grow steeper and taller until you're looking up at the Big Burn, Garrett Peak, and Mount Daly.

Nine miles above the T-intersection the road crosses Snowmass Creek, ¼ mile past that the road Ts again—the right fork goes .4 miles to the Forest Service parking lot and the end of the road. The left fork is a rough but mostly moderate 600', 1 ½-mile climb up to the Divide above Snowmass Village. For the long riders returning to Aspen, the climb over the Divide sets you up for a grand loop back along Owl Creek Road or the Government Trail (see Route #20).

29. Capitol Creek Road

Round Trip: (from Snowmass General Store) 20 miles, 2–3 hours
Elevation Gain: 2,800'
Difficulty: Beginner/Intermediate, Strenuous
Maps: p. 47

Notes: Capitol Creek Road, like Snowmass Creek Road, offers easy riding up a scenic valley, changing from a paved road to a gravel and then a dirt road. However, the last few miles of Capitol Creek Road requires some strenuous climbing to get to the wilderness trailhead and a view up the glacial valley to the dramatic north face of Capitol Peak. The lower part of Capitol Creek is as open a valley as you'll find so close to the high peaks—and with Mount Sopris and the Elk Mountain Ridge in front of you most of the way, and Capitol Peak framed in its valley at the end, the mountains are close indeed. As a result of this openness the valley is somewhat developed, but not nearly as much as it might have been; the valley residents blocked the development of a major ski area on Haystack Mountain—the wooded ridge with a rocky conical peak and bowl that you see ahead of you as you ride up the creek.

Access: (See Route #28)

Route: Follow Snowmass Creek Road south from the General Store; turn right onto Capitol Creek Road at the T-intersection 1 ¾ miles up the creek. Be aware of the occasional fast-traveling vehicle on this open road. The first 4 miles are flanked by hayfields, then the road climbs away from the creek and becomes gravel as it enters woods and begins the long, three-stage climb up to Cow Camp and the Capitol Creek trailhead. The road climbs up a final steep, ¼-mile hill past Cow Camp and wanders for a mile through the forest to its end at the Hardscrabble Lake trailhead—if you want that extra little bit to make your day.

Basalt

The Frying Pan River Valley is a special place, and not just for anglers. The rides up and out of the Frying Pan take you into a different country of deep, silent forests and weathered granite peaks. The rides are mostly long and smooth, and the climbing gradual. The "Around the Table" ride is by far the longest route in this book—just short of 100 miles of paved and dirt roads that takes you into beautiful, desert-like terrain in the Eagle River Valley and back again. To train for it, head out on the roads west of Basalt, and into the El Jebel and Carbondale areas.

30. Frying Pan River Road

Round Trip: It's up to you—the road goes all the way to Leadville
Elevation Gain: up to 7,000'
Difficulty: Beginner, Easy-Strenuous
Map: pp. 72-73

Notes: The Frying Pan River Road is a fully-paved county road and not a "mountain bike" route as such. On the other hand, the Frying Pan River is an extraordinarily beautiful mountain stream and well worth a leisurely inspection from the saddle of your bike—road or mountain. And when the backcountry is too wet or too far away for your time frame, it makes an ideal "training" ride—a long, easy climb upriver followed by a fast spin back down. That is, it's easy until you get to the base of Ruedi Dam, 13 miles upstream. Getting around the reservoir requires a strenuous 1,000' climb up onto the side of Red Table Mountain, followed by an 800' descent back to the river. This little excursion changes the nature of the ride from afternoon cruise to all-day commitment. Many riders make the bar in Thomasville (47 miles round trip) their turnaround point; the really obsessive carry on to the end of the pavement (63 miles round trip); and the aerobically possessed take it all the way to the 11,925' summit of Hagerman Pass (92 miles round trip).

Access: The Frying Pan River Road is the eastward extension of Midland Avenue, Basalt's main street; just keep going through town. If you drive to Basalt, use the RFTA park-and-ride lot south of the 7-11 store. This ride is not recommended for a summer weekend—too many people drive up the valley to go fishing, water-skiing, windsurfing, 4-wheeling, camping, hiking, mountain biking, etc. It's better to go on a weekday or during the off-seasons.

Lime kilns near Lime Creek on the Frying Pan River Road.

Route: Most of the first mile is occupied by the eastern outskirts of Basalt; beyond that the narrowness of the valley dictates that it be sparsely settled. The river is in view and accessible from the road most of the way up to the dam, with only a few steep banks and private property closures. Four miles up you come to the Seven Castles area, a widening of the valley overlooked by a series of sheer red sandstone buttresses. Nine miles up is another opening occupied by the beautiful Cap K Ranch. The valley grows a little wilder beyond the ranch; the rest of the way to the dam the road hugs the river on the right with steep, rocky hillsides on the left.

The steepest part of the climb is getting up the side of the canyon below the dam. Once past the dam the pitch eases off as the road winds upward through valleys and ridges. In the fall the aspen groves on this side of the valley wax golden while the opposite, north-facing slope stands in contrasting evergreen. The valley above the lake has a markedly more rugged feel—it opens up to embrace the higher peaks and the river becomes a rocky, rushing creek. Shortly past Thomasville the bedrock changes from warm red sandstone to greyish brown limestone to dark, obdurate granite. By the end of the paved road you're looking at high, rocky ridges jutting through the tree line not so far above you.

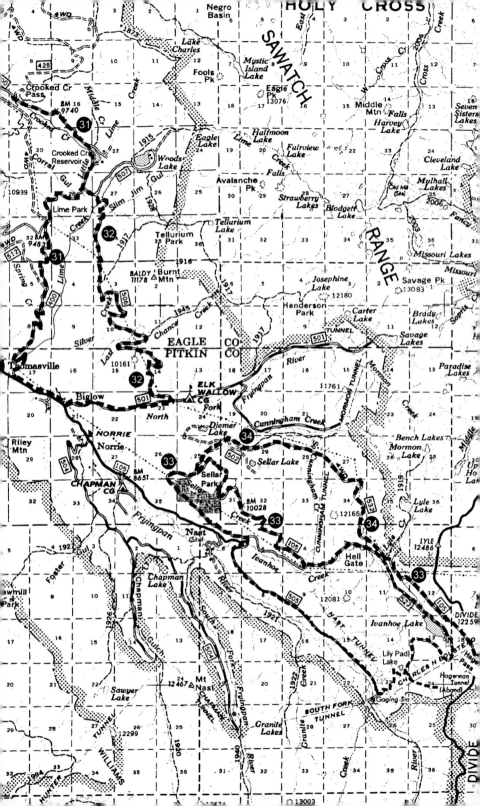

31. Lime Creek Road

Round Trip: (to Lime Park) 14 miles, 2–3 hours
(to Crooked Creek Pass) 22 ½ miles, 3–4 hours
Elevation Gain: 1,600'/2,150'
Difficulty: Beginner, Moderate/Strenuous
Map: p. 58

Notes: Lime Creek Road is a popular route between Thomasville on the Frying Pan River, and Lime Park and Crooked Creek Pass—especially in September when the aspen groves in Lime Park drape the hills with gold. The most spectacular mountain park in the Roaring Fork watershed, Lime Park is blessed with miles of undulating hills, the aforementioned aspen stands, its own limestone canyon, and a truly panoramic view of the granite peaks of the Sawatch Range—not to mention miles of dark timber around the park and Red Table Mountain behind it. A mile beyond the far end of the park is Crooked Creek Reservoir, a quiet little lake in its own little park; and 2 miles past that is the top of the pass. At 9,995' Crooked Creek Pass is not particularly noteworthy except as the gateway to epic rides around and over Red Table Mountain. In the middle of the park is the junction with Burnt Mountain Road (see Route #32), which offers a different and more challenging way back to the Frying Pan River Road.

Access: From Basalt, drive 24.7 miles up the Frying Pan River Road, past the Ruedi Reservoir, the small settlement of Meredith, and 1 ¼ miles past Thomasville to Lime Creek Road, which cuts back across the hillside on the left. You should be able to find some room for parking at the turnoff; one-tenth of a mile further up on the other side of the road is a picnic area.

Route: Climb easily around the end of a ridge and descend gently to cross Lime Creek near a small ranch. The road switches back up the other side of the creek, then winds along a ridge and into a side valley, Spring Creek. After crossing Spring Creek, 2 ½ miles in, the road begins climbing steeply up the side of a ridge; 1 ½ miles and three switchbacks later, most of your grunt work is behind you. The road just about levels off and ducks in and out of a couple of side gulches with glimpses of Lime Creek Canyon below. After rounding the second point you come out of the trees and Lime Park begins to open up before you; another ½ mile and the whole panorama is at your feet. The road runs level to the next side creek, then drops 300' over the course of a mile to Crooked Creek.

For a simple out-and-back tour, the top of the park is a natural place to turn around. The Burnt Mountain Road (see Route #32) forks right where Lime Creek Road meets Crooked Creek; a gentle mile up Crooked Creek is the reservoir. Beyond the reservoir the road begins climbing steadily again to the top of the pass. The numerous logging roads and jeep and pack trails around Lime Park are worthy of further exploration. Use the USGS quad maps as your starting point but remember that they aren't entirely accurate or up-to-date. And beware of logging trucks during summer working days if you get over onto the Eagle side of the pass.

To Eagle: On the north side of Crooked Creek Pass, the road drops steadily through aspen and spruce forest to Sylvan Lake, 4.3 miles past the summit. At the south end of the lake, Forest Road 414 joins the pass road from the left. Beyond Sylvan Lake the main road drops gradually down the narrow West Brush Creek Valley. Five miles down it joins the Yeoman Park Road from East Brush Creek (and the proposed Adams Rib ski area); shortly beyond that point it turns to pavement for the remaining ten miles of open ranch country into Eagle. From there it's a mere thirty-odd miles back along Route 6 and the Glenwood Canyon Bike Path to Glenwood Springs and the Roaring Fork Valley.

32. Burnt Mountain Loop

Round Trip: 21.5 miles, 3–5 hours
Elevation Gain: 3,000′
Difficulty: Intermediate, Strenuous
Map: p. 58

Notes: An over-hill-and-down-dale cruise through the woods taking the long way from Lime Park (see Route #31) back to the Frying Pan. A good workout, combining three good climbs with a couple of long descents and a few flats mixed in.

Access: (See Route #31). Follow Lime Creek Road to where the road drops down to meet Crooked Creek at mile 8. Turn right across the creek on Forest Road 506—Burnt Mountain Road.

Route: The road contours around the end of a ridge into the eastern end of Lime Park, where the Burnt Mountain Road forks right and drops down to Lime Creek. From the creek the road climbs eastward through the park, then loops back into the woods on the south side. Just before entering the woods you can look back across the head of the canyon to the western half of Lime Park. The climb crests briefly after ½ mile as you cross Slim Jim Gulch, then gently resumes for another ½ mile as you cross the meadow and enter the woods. After a dip to the creek bed below the Gates Hut, the climbing gets real as you gain 500' over the next long mile up the western shoulder of Burnt Mountain.

Now you get to lose everything you've just gained over the next two miles down to Last Chance Creek. But don't worry, you get it all back again over the next 1 ½ miles up over the western ridge of Savage Peak. The peak is well named—the forest is dark and dense and the cut across the north slope is the longest and steepest of the whole loop. The top, though, is the top and the last 6 miles are downhill: a couple of rocky ones down to the North Fork Road (turn right) onto a fast flat and then 2 miles of downhill gravel to the Frying Pan Road (right again), and the final 1 ¼-mile sprint back to the Lime Creek turnoff.

33. Hagerman Pass Road

Round Trip: (from end of paved Frying Pan Road) 29 miles, 3–5 hours
Elevation Gain: 2,700'
Difficulty: Beginner/Intermediate, Easy/Moderate
Map: p. 58

Notes: The first 10 ½ miles of the Hagerman Pass Road (Forest Road 105) follows the old Midland Railroad right-of-way, a gentle, steady climb up through the aspen and subalpine forests to the upper edge of the tree zone near Ivanhoe Lake. Almost anyone can ride this section; the final 4 miles diverge from the railroad grade to follow a jeep road that demands a little more effort and skill. Altogether, it's the easiest unpaved pass in this area. For a party of mixed abilities, there are variations and side routes to accommodate both beginner and expert, as well as a hiking trail (Lyle Lake) that starts at the turn off the railroad grade. If you're looking for a multiday ride, the Hagerman Pass Road leads down to Leadville on the east side of the Continental Divide; from there you can return over Hagerman Pass or continue on to the north, south, or east in search of further adventure.

Access: From downtown Basalt, follow the Frying Pan River Road (see Route #30) to the end of the pavement, 31.5 miles upstream. Here the road forks; take the left fork and park in the large parking area just around the corner, or drive the first 3.3 miles up to Sellar Park where there are a number of campsites and places to park.

On top of a continent at Hagerman Pass.

Route: From the parking area at the end of the Frying Pan Road, traverse west (left) along the side of the mountain toward Basalt. The tempting road that goes east up Ivanhoe Creek from the parking area dead-ends in the bottom of a deep canyon a few miles upstream. The traverse climbs gently and steadily for 2 ½ miles until the road crests out of the inner valley, crosses a small creek, and finally heads east toward the pass. Another ½ mile brings you to a magnificent, marshy meadow known as Sellar Park—a wildlife sanctuary with ruined coke ovens on the south side of the creek and long views across the forested Frying Pan Valley to the high peaks along the Continental Divide.

Here a spur road (Forest Road 502) forks left to Diemer and Sellar Lakes, a short side route in its own right and the return end of the Sellar Peak Road loop (see Route #34). The traverse around the park (and a smaller meadow above it) climbs almost imperceptibly for several miles along the west flank of Sellar Peak; as the road works its way back toward Ivanhoe Creek there are some open views south across the canyon to Mount Massive. Soon the canyon walls steepen to cliffs above and below the road—imagine yourself here in 1890, deep in the vast, rocky wilderness of Colorado, peering over the edge through the soot-stained window of a creaky wooden railway car. Once through the narrows, the scenery becomes distinctly alpine—open hillsides dotted with granite boulders and stunted trees above, a marshy, meandering creek flanked by dense willow thickets below. Another 1 ½ miles of sometimes rocky riding brings you to the Hagerman Pass/Ivanhoe Lake junction. The road straight ahead through the gate leads to Ivanhoe Lake and the old Hagerman Tunnel portal.

To go to the pass, turn left up a short, rocky hill to the Lyle Lake trailhead; the pass road bears right and traverses upward for ½ mile, then makes a few switchbacks up to another long, easy traverse above Ivanhoe Lake. A last set of switchbacks brings you up to the crest of the ridge and an easy runout to the summit of Hagerman Pass. The summit is broad and level, with long views east across the Arkansas Valley to the Mosquito Range. The ridge to the south rises gradually toward the summit of Mount Massive, the second highest peak in Colorado.

Extension to Hagerman Tunnel: On your return from Hagerman Pass (or in lieu of riding to the top), take the main road through the gate to Ivanhoe Lake and the old tunnel portal, 5 ¾ miles past the Ivanhoe/Hagerman junction. The first 2 ½ miles is almost level as you follow the graded road along the creek and the edge of the reservoir, then go left up a short, rough hill to regain the railroad grade. This section is not maintained like the lower part of the road, so it's a little more interesting riding with several stream crossings. After rounding the head of the lake, the grade heads northwest for about a mile, then rounds the end of a rocky ridge for a spectacular view of Lily Pad Lake nestled in the corner of another high mountain meadow. A mile further along the backside of the ridge a jeep road drops down to the right to access the lake. Just past that is a short rough section of road, ½ mile beyond that the sealed entrance to the once famous Hagerman Tunnel.

Frying Pan River Trail: For a truly spectacular—and exposed—return trip, take the Hagerman Tunnel Extension as far as the Lily Pad Lake turnoff. Drop down into the meadow and across it to the lake. Just past the lake the road drops over the side of the Frying Pan Valley, makes a few switchbacks and abruptly comes to an end. A faint trail continues on across the side of a near cliff (a carry for mortal riders) and disappears around the side of the mountain. If you can get safely across this section, which is constantly eroding, the iffy track becomes an old wagon road which switchbacks steeply down the mountainside to the water diversion intake on the Frying Pan. Pick up the well-maintained gravel road for a fast, 5-mile return to the start of pavement and the parking area. An equally challenging, and more strenuous, alternate return route is the Sellar Peak Road (See # 34).

34. Sellar Peak Road

One Way: (from Hagerman Pass/Ivanhoe Lake junction to paved Frying Pan Road) 11 miles, 2 hours
Elevation Gain: 1,200'
Difficulty: Advanced, Strenuous
Map: p. 58

Notes: For more advanced riders, the return ride down the Hagerman Pass Road can be a little boring. The Sellar Peak Road (Forest Road 532) offers a challenging alternative that adds ½ mile to the distance, an hour to the time, and an order of magnitude to the fun. It can also be done as a loop in its own right from the Frying Pan Road or Sellar Park without going to the top of the pass—just double the time and the distance.

Access: (See Route #33.) Descending from Hagerman Pass, turn right onto a rough jeep road just before reaching the Hagerman Pass/Ivanhoe Lake junction.

Coming up from the Frying Pan Road, turn left at the Hagerman Pass/Ivanhoe Lake junction, and immediately left again before reaching the Lyle Lake trailhead.

Route: The start of the Sellar Peak Road is difficult and rocky, then the grade eases and the road smooths out into a lovely alpine double track. As you approach the top of the saddle (1 ¼ miles) a series of short, challenging pitches interrupts the steady climb. Once over the saddle the road switchbacks down into Cunningham Creek for 2 miles of rough, cobbly fun to apparently end at a wide, smooth—and deserted—dirt road. Turn left onto this newer road, crank up a .4-mile hill,

Legacy of early railroaders along Sellar Peak Road.

cross an open flat and bear right onto the jeep track again as the dirt road turns sharply left to its end at one of the many water diversion structures that infest the Frying Pan Valley. The road drops a little, then climbs ¼ mile to the crest of a ridge before descending for a long, lovely mile through the lodgepole forest. Who goes down must go up again—the track climbs back up the side of the ridge again, sometimes steeply, for ¾ mile to end at Forest Road 502, three-quarters of a mile below Sellar Lake. Turn left to visit the lake, bear right for the 1 ½-mile descent back to Sellar Park and on to the Frying Pan Road. Immediately after the junction with Road 502, a road bears off to the right to Diemer Lake; ½ mile down the descent a second right heads down that way as well. Keep left at both, Diemer Lake is an off-route dead end.

35. Basalt Bike Path

Round Trip: 8 miles, ½–1 hour
Elevation Gain: 350'
Difficulty: Beginning, Easy/Moderate
Map: p. 66

Notes: Opened in 1994, the Basalt Bike Path filled the last gap in the main valley bike route. Now it's possible to ride from Aspen to Carbondale without having to ride on Highway 82 or go miles (and hundreds of feet of climbing) out of the way. It also makes possible a number of loop rides (such as Route #36), and for many people in Basalt is a quick, safe way to get out of town for some exercise. Like the Rio Grande Trail in Aspen, it has a large number of pedestrians, as well as cyclists, and many blind curves, so adjust your pace accordingly.

Access: From Midland Avenue in Basalt, ride ½ mile south along Two Rivers Road (Old Highway 82) to the last road on the left before reaching the new highway. The bike path begins on the south corner of this intersection. Coming towards Basalt from Woody Creek on the Lower River Road, keep going straight where the main road turns left to cross the bridge to Old Snowmass.

Route: The path starts parallel to the highway, then crosses a driveway and angles up the hillside to the left for half a mile to the upper tier of the Holland Hills subdivision. Where it meets a street, turn sharply downhill to your right, and then left on the next street. Follow this street ¼ mile to its end, then switchback left and right next to a house to regain the bike path proper, which leaves the subdivision and meanders along between a piñon covered, red rock hillside on the left and a hayfield on the right.

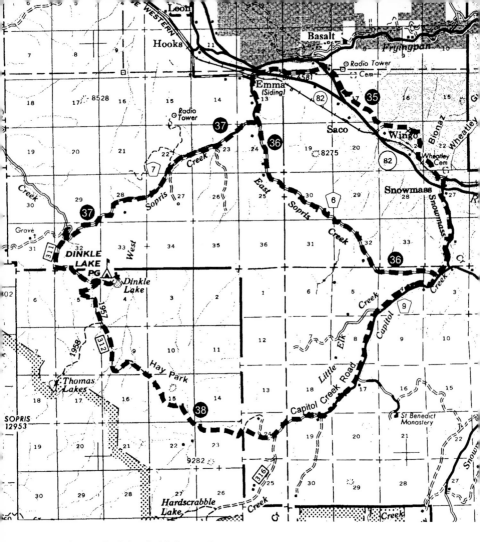

At the end of the field the path drops right down a short steep hill, climbs a little and then dips down toward the river and up again. The second dip, through dense oak scrub, has very poor sight lines and the pitches are steep enough to give out-of-shape riders a little trouble. After the dips the path begins meandering again through the fields and along the railroad track to its end at Old Snowmass. Turn right to cross the bridge and highway to the General Store and Snowmass Creek Road, or go straight ahead to follow the Lower River Road toward Woody Creek—a pleasant, easy country ride.

36. East Sopris Creek Road

Round Trip: (loop ride from Basalt) 14 ½ miles, 1–3 hours
Elevation Gain: 900'
Difficulty: Beginner, Easy/Moderate
Map: p. 66

Notes: While often incorporated into longer rides (Aspen-Carbondale, Aspen-Basalt and back), combined with the Basalt Bike Path and part of Snowmass Creek Road, East Sopris Creek makes for an excellent loop ride. The majority of the route is paved; the graveled road on the descent from the Little Elk Creek Divide to Emma adds just a touch of excitement to this scenic cruiser. Its main attractions are some lovely ranches along East Sopris Creek and the views of Mount Sopris. It can be ridden in either direction, though the climbing is significantly smoother and easier when ridden clockwise, as described here.

Access: From downtown Basalt, ride east along Two Rivers Road (Old Highway 82) to the Basalt Bike Path (see Route #35).

Route: Take the bike path all the way to the other end at the Lower River Road, turn right across the bridge and cross Highway 82 to the Snowmass General Store and Snowmass Creek Road. Follow Snowmass Creek Road (occasional heavy traffic) 1 ¾ miles to the T-intersection with Capitol Creek Road. Turn right onto Capitol Creek Road for .3 miles, then fork right again onto East Sopris Creek Road (County Road 7). The road drops down to Capitol Creek and makes a short, steep climb up out of the creek bed. From here the road runs straight across the pasture land above Little Elk Creek, climbing gently toward East Sopris Creek Divide with panoramic views of the Elk Mountain Ridge and Mount Sopris.

After rounding a few bends, the road crosses the divide and begins its descent toward Emma. The first mile is straight and gentle, then the hills get steeper and the turns sharper all the way to the junction with West Sopris Creek Road (the mountain bike route to Carbondale; see Route #37). Turn right here; Sopris Creek Road ends a mile further on with a left-hand turn onto the Emma Road. Turn right again almost immediately and cross Highway 82 to the bike path on the other side. If the traffic is too heavy, or you're not comfortable crossing the 4-lane highway, just go left onto the bike path along your side of the highway—it will cross under the highway and come back up along the other side. Once on the other side of Highway 82, follow the frontage road (which quickly turns into a bike path) past the old brick building for a pleasant 1 ½-mile cruise back to Basalt.

37. West Sopris Creek Road to Dinkle Lake

Round Trip: (from Basalt) 20 miles, 2–4 hours
Elevation Gain: 2,000′
Difficulty: Beginner, Moderate
Map: p. 66

Notes: West Sopris Creek Road is a fine cruise or training ride in itself—it's also the access to the Hay Park Trail (see Route #38), and links East Sopris Creek Road (Route #36) to Prince Creek Road (Route #52) to form the backbone of the Aspen-Carbondale back road route. The climb is steady and rarely demanding and is dominated by views of Mount Sopris brooding over the forest at its feet.

Access: Coming out of Basalt, cross the bridge behind the 7-11 store as if you were headed to Highway 82 and Aspen. Just before the light, turn right onto the old Emma Road which turns into a bike path after ½ mile. Follow the bike path another mile until it re-merges into the old road that turns left to intersect the highway. You can either cross on the highway or follow the bike path another hundred yards to a bike underpass and come back up to the road on the other side. Once across the highway and the railroad tracks turn left for 100 yards and then right onto Sopris Creek Road. Follow this road for just over a mile until the road comes to a T—West Sopris Creek Road is the right branch of the T.

Mount Sopris looms above the brushy roadside on West Sopris Creek.

Route: The West Sopris Creek Road crosses the level creek bottom and then begins to climb up a draw. After 1 ¼ miles the pavement gives way to gravel (landowners are lobbying the county to extend the pavement further); climb up around a tight S-curve and the valley begins to open up. The pitch eases off and you can enjoy the ride and the views of well-kept ranches and Mount Sopris for the next several miles. A hairpin turn to the right starts the final ¼-mile pitch to the Prince Creek Divide. At the crest of the ridge, fork left onto Forest Road 311 to ride the final 2 miles to Dinkle Lake and the Thomas Lakes/Hay Park trailhead (see Route #38), or go straight ahead to Prince Creek Road and Carbondale (see Route #52), or turn right onto the demanding double and single tracks of the Crown Trails (see Route #54).

The Dinkle Lake Road (Forest Road 311) is narrower and rougher than the main road, though still within the range of novice riders. It follows the ridge line through dense scrub oak for ¾ mile, then turns left and traverses up through aspen forest and meadows to the trailhead parking for Thomas Lakes/Hay Park. Dinkle Lake itself, a popular picnic spot and fishing hole, is ¼ mile down the hill past the parking area.

38. Hay Park Trail

Round Trip: (from Thomas Lakes Trailhead) 8 miles, 2–3 hours
(loop: Basalt–Hay Park–Capitol Cr.–Basalt) 30 miles, 4–6 hrs.
Elevation Gain: 1,200'/3,200'
Difficulty: Advanced/Expert, Strenuous
Map: p. 66

Notes: Hay Park (Trail 1957) can be done as either a modest out-and-back ride or as the centerpiece of a gonzo, 30-mile loop. The park itself is a lovely, isolated meadow among the aspen stands, marred only by the presence (or signs) of numerous cattle. The route offers some fine single-tracking that ranges from smooth and sweet to problematic (mostly on the longer loop). With two vehicles you could also set up a shuttle by parking one at the Thomas Lakes/Hay Park trailhead and the other at the Capitol Creek end to do the single track. It could be ridden either way, though north to south seems more natural, with no significant uphill pushes.

Access: (See Route #37.) If driving to the trailhead, go west on Highway 82 from the Basalt stoplight 1 ½ miles. Just past the crest of the hill above the Roaring Fork River bridge, turn left onto the Emma Road—a turning lane but no highway sign. From here follow the bike route directions (see

Route #37) to the trailhead parking lot. Parking is on the left, the trailhead is on the right.

Route: Ride directly up the hill to intersect an old road, which you will follow for the next 3 miles. The first mile is the hardest part—not terribly steep, but much of it covered with loose, fist-sized rocks that will test your leg power and balance and steering skills. If you have trouble, you can push through the worst parts without losing much of the ride. Shortly after things smooth out there's a good lookout over Dinkle Lake and the Roaring Fork Valley. About ½ mile further on, the hiking trail to Thomas Lakes spurs right off the road—keep going straight ahead into the woods. This last section is underlain by shale beds, and turns to a slick, black gumbo with the slightest moisture. Be forewarned.

The next 1 ¼ miles is a pure pleasure ride through aspen groves and meadows, climbing maybe a 2% grade. At the 3-mile point the road crosses West Sopris Creek on a loose log "bridge." Immediately after the crossing bear left onto a single track which descends a short hill to merge with a pack trail coming up from Dinkle Lake. Keep going south and east on this trail to emerge into Hay Park ½ mile after leaving the road. If you want to hang out, this is the area to do it before turning around.

To continue on the loop to Capitol Creek, cross a seasonal creek and head south along the edge of some aspen stands, then up a hill to a gate through the fence that runs along its top. Through this section and for the next couple of miles there are many cowpaths or abandoned trail segments—take the time to make sure you're on the right track.

From the top of the hill the trail goes down through some brush into the aspen, heading generally toward Capitol Peak. Mostly smooth, it traverses and descends, traverses, descends, and climbs as it works its way across the grain of the land with just enough obstacles and technical difficulties to keep you on your toes. After 2 miles of fun among the aspen, the trail gets a little funkier with more obstacles, mud, stream crossings, and an uphill trend. Then it smooths out and starts heading downward again for a mile to merge with a private dirt road. Turn right for .2 mile, and climb right up the bank off the road. Crest over a rise, cross the same road again, and descend ¾ mile to the trailhead at Capitol Creek Road.

Turn left here; after a fast 1 ½ miles on the dirt the road goes to chipseal. Stay on Capitol Creek Road for 6 ½ miles to the T-intersection with Snowmass Creek Road. Turn left at the T and take Snowmass Creek Road 1 ¾ miles to Highway 82. Cross the highway onto Lower River Road; immediately after the bridge across the Roaring Fork turn left onto the Basalt Bike Path for a wandering, rolling 4-mile ride back to town.

39. Around the Table

Round Trip: (loop) 93 miles, a full day
Elevation Gain: 7,500'
Difficulty: Beginner(!?), Strenuous
Map: pp. 72-73

Notes: The mileage is a little short and, yes, it's 40% pavement, but this is a mountain bike century ride, pure and simple. From Basalt to Catherine Store, over Cottonwood Pass almost to Gypsum, up Gypsum Creek and over Hardscrabble Mountain to Sylvan Lake, over Crooked Creek Pass to Thomasville, and down the Frying Pan to Basalt again: it's a monster loop that will imprint in your bones the size of the country we live in. Pump up your tires and do it.

Access: Downtown Basalt. Park in the RFTA park-and-ride south of the 7-11 store.

Route: Take Two Rivers Road (Old Highway 82) west along the river to the Highway 82 stoplight (2 miles), cross the highway to Willits Lane. Continue along the river to the Hooks Lane Bridge, bear right on Willits Lane almost back to Highway 82. Turn left onto the frontage road for the City Market shopping complex, go past the stores to the El Jebel light (4 ¼ cumulative miles). Instead of turning right to the light, keep going straight on Valley Road until it bears around to the right to meet Highway 82 (5 ½ miles). Just before the intersection turn left onto another frontage road (Old Highway 82 again) to Catherine Store (8 miles). Turn right, cross the highway and begin climbing up to Missouri Heights on Catherine Store Road (County Road 100). The first 1 ½ miles involve some steep climbing, the next 2 ½ gently climb and roll to the crest of a ridge above Cattle Creek. Drop down to the creek and pick up the Cottonwood Pass Road (County Road 113) which becomes gravel at this point (12 ¾ miles). Follow it past Coulter Creek Road (on the left) and Upper Cattle Creek Road (on the right). After running along the bottom of Shippee's Draw, the road climbs steeply through some loose switchbacks for 1 ½ miles to parallel East Coulter Creek for several miles. Another short climb leads you to the Cottonwood Divide (21 miles).

From the top of the divide the road winds steeply down to Cottonwood Creek for 2 miles and follows the creek bed for 1 ½ miles before crossing it and climbing ½ mile of steep, loose turns to the top of the Spring Gulch Divide (25 ½ miles). From here you plunge down into the wide, fertile Gypsum Creek Valley, steeply at first and then on a long runout until you hit pavement just before reaching the creek. Turn right, cross

the creek, and immediately bear left onto Daggett Lane which will run you straight across the fields to Valley Road (30 ½ miles). Turn right for 2 straight miles up the valley, then the road (Forest Road 412) begins winding into Gypsum Creek Canyon which it follows for about 8 miles of gradual climbing. At the end of the canyon the road bends eastward and the valley opens up into a big willowy wetland. On the left is the barren southern face of Hardscrabble Mountain, to the right the lush, forested north slope of Red Table Mountain. The climb steepens after about 4 miles; in another 1 ¼ miles turn left onto Hardscrabble Mountain Road (Forest Road 411) for a moderately steep climb to its junction with West Brush Creek Road (Forest Road 414—47 ¼ miles). Turn right onto Road 414 for a wonderful rolling, winding 5 ½-mile descent (with some intermittent climbs) to Sylvan Lake. Just above Sylvan Lake turn right onto Forest Road 400 (53 miles) for a moderate, 4 ¼-mile climb to the top of Crooked Creek Pass (57 ¼ miles).

Most of the work is over now. A fast 2 ¼-mile descent takes you past Crooked Creek Reservoir to the junction with Burnt Mountain Road (Forest Road 506). Keep right for a mile of easy climbing up to the top of Lime Park, then the 7-mile descent to the Frying Pan Road (68 ½ miles). Back on pavement it's more downhill past Thomasville and Meredith to the head of Ruedi Reservoir and one last, thankless 600' climb to get around the reservoir. The next 4 miles are a fast downhill back to the Frying Pan River and a 13-mile cruise home to Basalt (93 ¼ miles).

Heading up Gypsum Creek toward Red Table Mountain, Around-the-Table route.

El Jebel

Midvalley riding around El Jebel, up onto Missouri Heights, and on Basalt Mountain is back road riding at its best—lots of long, smooth miles with some good medium-sized climbs and not much traffic. Most of the rides are below 8,000' with a southern exposure for good early spring and late fall training. There are only a couple of single tracks in this section, but they're among the best around, and riding Red Table Mountain is a must for gonzo distance riders.

40. Upper Cattle Creek Road

Round Trip: 19 miles, 2–3 hours
Elevation Gain: 1,200'
Difficulty: Beginner, Moderate
Map: p. 76

Notes: Missouri Heights is a large bench 800' above the Roaring Fork River that extends northwest from Basalt Mountain towards Carbondale and Glenwood Springs. Partly ranched and partly subdivided, partly paved and partly dirt, it's laced with roads that are great for early and late season rides when the higher country is cold and wet. This route and the two following use some of these roads to create fun, interesting routes; a number of other combinations are possible as well, especially if you're willing to spend a little time riding on the shoulder of Highway 82. Upper Cattle Creek Road is a good workout loop with an emphasis on climbing, especially if ridden counterclockwise, in which case it rates "strenuous." The description below reads clockwise, which gives you a good downgrade warm-up and a more gradual ascent.

Access: The route starts at the El Jebel stoplight near the 19-mile marker on Highway 82. If you're coming by car, turn off on the north side and park in one of the many lots in the business center there.

Route: From El Jebel, cross over to the south side of Highway 82 at the light and immediately turn right on Valley Road. Follow this for 1 ¼ miles until it comes back to the highway. Just before the intersection turn left onto the old 2-lane highway, now a frontage road. Follow it for 2 ½ miles to its end at Catherine Store. Turn right and cross the highway onto County Road 100 (Catherine Store Road), which almost immediately begins climbing up out of the valley. A short steep hill leads you onto a ½-mile flat that goes back into the draw, another winding ½-mile hill gets you up onto the rolling flats of Missouri Heights. The flats last for 2 ¼ miles, then the road climbs over a low ridge and drops down into Cattle Creek where the pavement—and Catherine Store Road—end at the junction with Cattle Creek Road (County Road 113).

Follow Cattle Creek Road for 1 ½ miles toward Cottonwood Pass, then fork right onto Upper Cattle Creek Road (County Road 122), past the lush pastures and hayfields that line the creek bottom for another 1 ½ miles until the road leaves the creek and begins climbing up a draw toward Spring Park. Turn right at the junction with Basalt Mountain Road and enjoy the 2-mile cruise along the edge of Spring Park Reservoir. Soon after the pavement resumes the road drops off into a steep, winding 3-mile descent back to El Jebel.

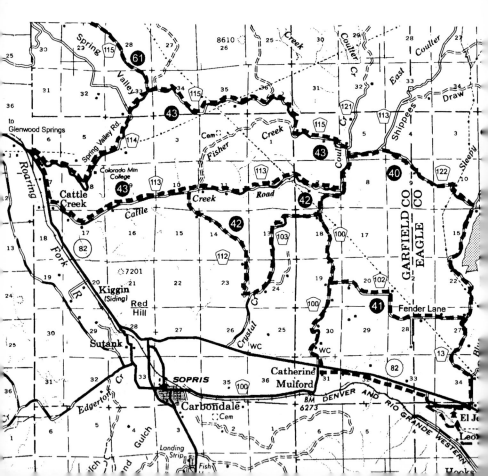

41. Fender Lane

Round Trip: 12 miles, 1–2 hours
Elevation Gain: 1,000'
Difficulty: Beginner, Moderate
Map: p. 76

Notes: A shorter version of the previous route, Fender Lane (County Road 102) can also be combined with the upper part of the Upper Cattle Creek ride to create a 13-mile loop entirely on Missouri Heights.

Access: (See Route #40)

Route: Follow the Upper Cattle Creek route (see Route #40) up onto the Heights; ¾ mile after cresting the hill turn right onto Road 102. For 1 ½ miles the road climbs gently through a series of right-angle doglegs as it works its way around a shallow ridge. After rounding the ridge it reverts to gravel (for a mile) and drops into a wide, grassy swale, then climbs moderately over another hill to join the Upper Cattle Creek Road 2 ¼ miles above El Jebel. Turn right to return to El Jebel.

42. Crystal Springs/Cattle Creek Loop

Round Trip: (from Catherine Store) 18 miles, 2–3 hours.
Elevation Gain: 2,300'
Difficulty: Beginner, Strenuous
Map: p. 76

Notes: Who says you have to climb big hills to burn your legs? Lots of little ones will do just as well, maybe better. This little stinker is designed with that specifically in mind—when you can't get to the big hills you make the little ones work for you. It combines four different roads to create a route that has only ¾ mile of dirt, but with enough variety and rough enough chipseal to make you happy to be on your mountain bike.

Access: The route starts at Catherine Store, on Highway 82 halfway between Carbondale and El Jebel. To ride the easy 3 ¾ miles from El Jebel, see Route #40. To ride from Carbondale, take County Road 100 east off of Main Street 3 ½ miles to Catherine Store.

Route: From Catherine Store, cross the highway on the Catherine Store Road (Road 100), which almost immediately begins climbing up out of the valley. A short steep hill leads you onto a ½-mile flat that goes back into the draw; another winding ½-mile hill gets you up onto the rolling flats of Missouri Heights. Roll across the Heights for 2 ¼ miles, then take a left onto Crystal Springs Road (County Road 103) at the base of a low ridge. The road parallels the ridge for ¾ mile, then turns to gravel for ¾ mile as it works through some right angle turns and heads toward Mount Sopris. The pavement resumes at the base of a knoll; crank over the knoll and start your descent. After descending gradually for a mile, the pitch steepens for another ½ mile to the junction with County Road 112. Make a hard right turn onto Road 112, and immediately start climbing steeply for ½ mile. The climb eases off for another ½ mile, then the road rolls along through the fields for another mile before beginning its descent into Cattle Creek at the 2-mile marker. The descent starts gradually, then winds very steeply (for a paved road) through a narrow cut towards the bottom. Cross the creek and turn right onto Cattle Creek Road (County Road 113) for a 4-mile climb back to the upper end of Catherine Store Road (Road 100). The climb steepens between the 4- and 6-mile markers on Cattle Creek Road, then levels off to the junction. Turn right on Road 100, push up the last hill, and coast (most of) the 4 miles back to Catherine Store.

43. Spring Valley Loop

Round Trip: 19 miles, 2–3 hours
Elevation Gain: 1,700'
Difficulty: Beginner, Moderate
Map: p. 76

Notes: The Spring Valley Loop is a long cruise through the least populous part of the Heights—lots of wild scrubland (very colorful in the fall) and saturation views of Sopris and the Elks. The first 3 miles follow a well-used paved road up to the Colorado Mountain College (CMC), the next 12 miles are as wild as it gets on county roads.

Access: Turn east at the CMC stoplight at mile 6.7 on Highway 82, halfway between Carbondale and Glenwood Springs. Park in the shopping plaza and start riding straight up the hill.

Route: The road immediately bears right and begins a long, steep, winding climb across a dry hillside. Half a mile up the road enters the piñon-juniper forest and turns away from the valley floor. Another mile up you crest the ridge for a view of Mount Sopris; at 2 miles you're on the level having disposed of half the climbing. The next mile is a pleasant cruise through the piñon and past the CMC campus. Bear 90 degrees left and off the pavement into Spring Valley just past the main entrance to the college. After another ¾ mile the road begins climbing a hill away from the valley floor; another ½ mile brings you to Red Canyon Road (County Road 115; see Route #61). Go right on Road 115, rolling through undeveloped sage and oak brush country with spectacular views of the Elk Mountains to the south.

This goes on for 3 miles until you cross the height of the land and begin dropping toward Coulter Creek, with views of Red Table and Basalt mountains (prime country for more serious riding) across the way. The descent steepens through a draw after a mile, then the road shoots out across the Coulter Creek flood plain to its junction with Coulter Creek Road (County Road 121). Turn right and join Cattle Creek Road (County Road 113) in a quarter mile, bear right ¾ mile down the hill (where the pavement starts) to follow Cattle Creek 7 miles back to Highway 82. Turn right on Highway 82 and ride the shoulder just over a mile back to your starting point. This route can be ridden the other way, though the climb turns into a long grind with some steep gravel at the end.

44. Cottonwood Pass Road

Round Trip: 26 miles, 2–4 hours
Elevation Gain: 2,000′
Difficulty: Beginner, Moderate
Maps: pp. 72, 82

Notes: Cottonwood Pass Road is a little-used back route between the Roaring Fork and Eagle valleys, closed in the winter and "impassable when wet"—as a sign along the way advises the unwary traveler. A few miles out of the main valleys and you're back in the rural West of dry, scrubby rangeland fringed by aspen stands and framed by dark-timbered mountains. You can feel the harsh loneliness of the land as well as its beauty, and understand the fierce independence it bred among its people. The tourist age intrudes, but does not dominate. For an easier ride, you can drive just past the end of pavement to the Coulter Creek junction; for gonzo rides go on over the pass to the Red Table (see Route #47) and Around the Table (see Route #39).

Access: From Catherine Store on Highway 82, halfway between El Jebel and Carbondale, take Catherine Store Road (County Road 100) north up the hill. To ride the easy 3 ¾ miles from El Jebel, see the description in Route #40. To start from Carbondale take Catherine Store Road (Road 100) from the east end of Main Street 3 ½ miles to Catherine Store. From Glenwood Springs, turn left onto Cattle Creek Road (Road 113) at the

7.8 mile point on Highway 82. Park in the shopping plaza there and ride, or drive the gradually climbing (7 miles, 1,000' elevation gain) chipseal road to Cottonwood Pass Road. Turn left, park at the junction with Coulter Creek Road ¾ mile on.

Route: The Catherine Store Road almost immediately begins climbing up out of the valley. A short steep hill leads you onto a ½-mile flat that goes back into the draw; another winding ½-mile hill gets you up onto the gently rising flats of Missouri Heights. The flats last for 2 ¼ miles, then the road climbs over a low ridge and drops down into Cattle Creek, where the pavement—and Catherine Store Road—end at the junction with Cattle Creek Road (County Road 113). Keep straight ahead up a short hill, bear right at the junction with Coulter Creek Road (County Road 121). Another ¾ mile past the beaver ponds on Cattle Creek Road brings you to the junction with Upper Cattle Creek Road (County Road 13). Stay left and ride for a mile along Shippee's Draw, then begin climbing the switchbacks up onto the rangeland. Once out of the draw the road follows East Coulter Creek for about 3 miles before one last climb up onto the Cottonwood Divide. Ride another mile on the flat to where the road begins descending toward Cottonwood Creek. Stop here, you're at the end of the route.

Cow country near the top of Cottonwood Pass.

45. Basalt Mountain Road

Round Trip: (from Forest Service parking) 10 ½ miles, 1 ½ –3 hours/
(from El Jebel) 25 miles, 3–5 hours
Elevation Gain: 1,750'/3,150'
Difficulty: Beginner, Strenuous
Map: p. 82

Notes: Basalt Mountain is to midvalley, roughly, what Smuggler Mountain is to Aspen—a quick escape route into the backcountry. Not the most spectacular ride you'll ever do, but one that can quickly become an old favorite. The road itself is a well-maintained Forest Service access road to timber sales on top of the mountain—sales that are now on hold because of its popularity as a recreation area.

Access: Turn north off of Highway 82 at the El Jebel light. Park here or at the Forest Service lot 7 ½ miles up the road at the base of the peak. Go straight towards the Missouri Heights bluffs on El Jebel Road, which becomes Upper Cattle Creek Road. The road runs flat for .7 miles, then cuts left across the face of the bluff and climbs 800' over the next 1 ¾ miles—a real grind for pavement riding. At 3 ¼ miles the road finally flattens out and turns to dirt as it winds around Spring Park Reservoir. Near the far end of the reservoir where Upper Cattle Creek Road turns left, stay on Forest Road 509 which goes straight ahead and around the north end of the reservoir. A long mile of moderate climbing brings you to the Forest Service parking lot, at the intersection of roads 509 and 524.

Route: Road 509 bears left over a slight saddle at the parking lot and drops down into Cattle Creek; Basalt Mountain Road (Forest Road 524) circles around the end of the lot and starts up Basalt Mountain. Follow Basalt Mountain Road; the first 1 ½ miles is a gentle to moderate climb up the west face of Basalt Mountain with views across the reservoir to Mount Sopris and the Crystal River Valley. The rest of the way the road winds back and forth between the north and west faces of the mountain, mostly in the aspen and spruce/fir forest with occasional glimpses out toward Red Table Mountain or the Roaring Fork Valley. Just before the end the road climbs steeply between some boulder fields, then crosses a cattle guard to a rough parking area. From here you can access Trail 1909 (see Route #46) via a spur trail that begins on the left side of the parking area.

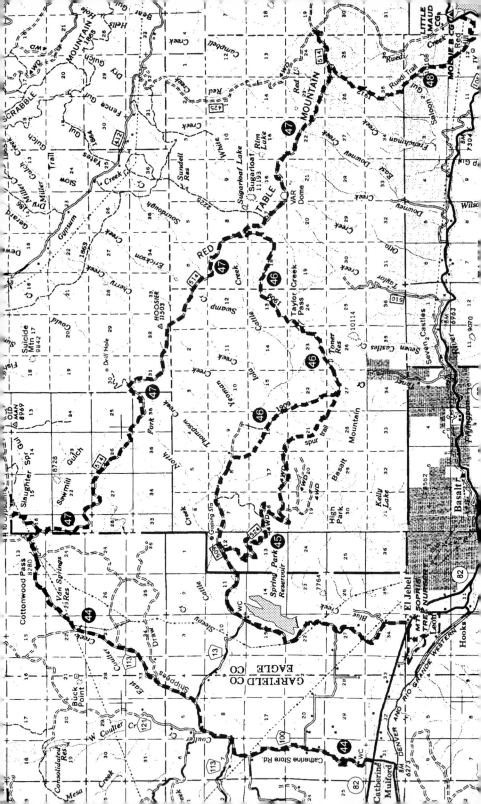

46. Trail 1909

Round Trip: (Basalt Mountain–Red Table) 25 miles, 4–6 hours/
　　　　　　　(Cattle Creek Loop) 15 miles, 3–5 hours
Elevation Gain: 2,600'/2,100'
Difficulty: Advanced, Strenuous
Map: p. 82

Notes: Officially, Trail 1909 runs from Cattle Creek to Red Table
Mountain. Practically, much of the lower section up the north side of
Basalt Mountain is too steep to climb. Happily, there is a spur trail from
the end of the Basalt Mountain Road (see Route #45) that eases the trip
up Red Table and creates a fine little loop ride down to Cattle Creek as
well. The spur is a bit of a boulder-hopping jumble, but the entirety of
Trail 1909 has recently been reconfigured with mountain bikes in mind,
making it one of the sweetest trails around.

Access: (See Route #45) To do the Red Table out-and-back route, drive
to the top of Basalt Mountain on Road 524 and ride out and back. To do
the Cattle Creek Loop, it works best to park at the lower Basalt Mountain
parking lot at the junction of Forest Roads 509 and 524, ride up Basalt
Mountain on Road 524 and back around on Trail 1909.

Route: From the trailhead sign at the end of the Basalt Mountain Road,
the spur trail begins as a jeep road gently descending through meadows
slightly scarred by logging. At .6 miles turn left at arrow post and "No
Motorized Vehicles" sign onto a rough 4-wheel drive track—the road
curves off to right. Wind through the woods for ¼ mile to the first rock
garden, where you can easily cross up your front wheel if you hit one of
the boulders wrong. The trail then forks, go left into more rock gardens;
the trail gradually smooths out and begins climbing around to the right
after a few hundred yards. One-half mile of intermittent climbing, more
technical than steep, brings you to another junction and another left turn.
Another ¾ mile of smoother riding brings you to a meadow and a stock
tank; the trail bears right around the pond and continues on a ½-mile
moderate, but technically interesting, climb through the meadow. At the
top of the climb the trail bears left through the woods for ¾ mile of fun
single-tracking, mostly downhill, to a long meadow surrounded by
lodgepole, and to the junction with Trail 1909 proper. Turn left to return
to Cattle Creek; turn right to Toner Reservoir and Red Table.

To Red Table: Climb gently out of the right side of the meadow for ¼
mile to another meadow that slopes northeast toward Toner Reservoir; a
lovely, winding descent of 1 ¼ miles through the woods and meadows

brings you to the reservoir. Cross the dam at the south end of the reservoir, contour around the east bank, and bear right up a draw into the woods for a mile of gentle climbing to the first knoll. Drop down the backside for glimpses of the Frying Pan Valley through the trees, then begin a ½-mile switchbacking climb up to the second knoll. From here you can see out to Red Table Mountain, seemingly within your grasp. Don't' be deceived—you still have 2 miles of trail and 3 miles of road to get to the top, 1,000' above you.

Drop down the back side of the knoll and begin climbing the ridge ahead of you. The trail slabs around to the east side for wide open views up the Frying Pan, then makes a short, steep drop to begin the last, long climb up Red Table proper. The first mile switchbacks up the side of the mountain, then breaks out onto the ridgetop and contours around the side of a wide, grassy gulch for ½ mile to the end of the single track at a roadhead. Follow the road straight ahead into the woods for ½ mile to its junction with the Taylor Creek Road (closed at private property line 3 miles down). Turn sharply left for a 1 ¼-mile climb up the ridge line and traverse around the head of the gulch the final mile to Red Table Road.

If you have the time and the energy (and haven't left your only car sitting on top of Basalt Mountain), you can ride 5 ½ miles east along the ridge to the Ruedi Trail (see Route #48) for perhaps the best single track descent around (and a 15-mile road ride back to Basalt).

To Cattle Creek: From the junction of the spur trail and Trail 1909 go left into the woods on Trail 1909. The descent starts gently then drops off into some tight switchbacks and a couple of short steeps, then begins traversing west across the mountainside with a lot of interesting ups and downs in and out of streambeds (be careful of the crossings). After 3 ½ miles it switches back to the right and follows a fence line down to Forest Road 509 and a parking lot across the road. Go left on Road 509 for a fast 2-mile run back to the lower Basalt Mountain parking lot—mostly downhill with two short climbs.

The rugged north slope of Red Table Mountain.

47. Red Table Road

Round Trip: (to radar dome) 26 miles, 4–6 hours
One Way: (to Trail 1909) 11 ¾ miles, 2–3 hours/ (to Ruedi Trail) 17 ¼
miles, 3–4 hours/ (to Red Creek Trail) 18 ½ miles, 3–4 hours
Elevation Gain: 4,000′
Difficulty: Intermediate, Strenuous
Map: p. 82

Notes: Red Table Mountain is the long, scalloped, red ridge that
dominates the northern horizon from anywhere in the Aspen/Snowmass
area. As the divide between the Roaring Fork and Eagle River watersheds
it offers 40-mile views in all directions—and a spectacular, demanding
ride. The ridge is 15 miles long; the road runs along the top for 10, and
it's an 8 ½-mile ride to get up there. Not a ride for the weak-kneed or
short-winded, it's a mother of a road that connects to some memorable
descent/alternate ascent routes: Trail 1909 (see Route #46), Ruedi Trail
(see Route #48), and Red Creek Road.

Access: (See Route #44). From the top of Cottonwood Pass descend
¾ mile and make a sharp right onto Red Table Road (Forest Road 514).
Watch for a small sign at the junction, which you come upon very
suddenly as you round a left-hand turn. You can park ¼ mile down the
road by the creek.

Route: The Red Table Road route consists of a long, gradual climb from 8,000' to 11,500', followed by a 10-mile run along the ridge. The best views are toward the end. For the first 2 miles the climb is steady but moderate through the gambel oak; after the first mile there are views out to Basalt Mountain and the Elk Range. The next 2 miles wander along the top of a ridge through the aspen forest without climbing very much; from 4 miles on the road gets into some real upward mobility, grinding steadily through 2,000' over 4 miles. As you approach the top of the ridge the forest breaks up into scattered stands interspersed with meadows; as you start along the ridge, the ground suddenly drops away on the north side into the deep glacial bowls of Cherry and Erickson lakes. Red Table Mountain is one of the lowest mountains where you'll see such dramatic signs of glaciation.

The ridge is a series of low peaks and saddles; from where you first gain the ridge, the road drops gradually for 1 ½ miles, then rolls along for another 1 ½ miles before climbing 600' over the next 1 ½ miles to the Red Table Radar Dome. One-third mile up this hill the road to Trail 1909 takes off to the right, marked by a post with a bike symbol and a sign reading "Locked Gate, 6 miles" (the gate is on the road—the trail takes a side road to the right 2 miles down). Three-quarters mile past the dome, the road dips down to a narrow neck with deep basins on both sides; in the northern basin is the little glacier-carved peak known as Sugarloaf, with its lake beside it.

A short steep climb takes you up onto the next ridge, followed by a 1 ½-mile descent to East Downey Creek, 1 ¼ miles of easy climbing to the next peak, and ¾ mile down to the next saddle. Four-tenths mile down on the right, marked by a small weathered sign, is the start of the Ruedi Trail (see Route #48), a 9-mile single track descent that spits you out onto the Frying Pan Road just above the Ruedi Dam. One-and-a-half miles past the Ruedi Trail junction, over the next little hill and 500' down to a low saddle, is a 4-way road junction. To the left is Red Creek Road (Forest Road 425), a lovely 8-mile jeep road down to Gypsum Creek; to the right is Ruedi Creek Road which runs down into private land. The Red Table Road goes on ahead for another mile before becoming a pack trail that goes all the way to Crooked Creek Pass—10 miles that no one we know has attempted.

48. Ruedi Trail

One Way: 8 ¾ miles, 1–2 hours down/2–3 hours up
Elevation Loss/Gain: 3,800′
Difficulty: Advanced/Expert, Strenuous
Map: p. 82

Notes: The Ruedi Trail is a great single track popular with motorcyclists which is a little hard to get to for mountain bikers. Riding up it is mostly enjoyable. The top mile, though, is mostly pushing over boulder fields. Descending it is a wonderful way to cap a long day's climb up onto Red Table via various routes—Red Table Road (see Route #47), Trail 1909 (see Route #46), or Red Creek Road. Most of the trail is smooth single-tracking down a long ridge through the aspen forest, with a lot of rocks near the top and some minor technicalities further down.

Access: Just under 16 miles from Basalt up the Frying Pan River Road, the Ruedi Trail goes left into the woods opposite the campground/marina just above the Ruedi Reservoir Dam. See Route #47 for access from the top.

Route (from the top): Turn south onto single track, which switches back and forth across rocky terrain for a mile, entailing numerous dismounts. After entering the forest it smooths out for the most part. About 3 ½ miles down it switches back onto the east side of the ridge, requiring some sidehill riding and offering open views of Ruedi Reservoir. For the next couple of miles it cuts back onto the top of the broad ridge and into aspen for smooth, soft riding. Many switchbacks keep the angle low, and most of them are negotiable, the main challenge being motorcycle ruts. At 6 miles the trail merges with a power-line service road and climbs a short hill, then veers left onto a single track again to a spectacular overlook directly above the dam and Rocky Fork Creek. From here the trail works back along the east face of the ridge through deep spruce/fir forest; 1 ¾ miles down it passes under the power line again, switchbacks into a road, and immediately drops left onto single track again, which ends ½ mile later at the Frying Pan Road.

Carbondale/Crystal River Valley

Mountain bike rides are sparse right around Carbondale—you can go up Prince Creek Road to the Porcupine Loop, the Crown Trails, or Hay Park—but the Crystal River Valley has some classics. Tall Pines and the Ragged Mountain Trail are memorable trail rides, and Schofield Pass and Lead King Basin offer alpine scenery at its best.

49. Thompson Creek Road

Round Trip: 14 miles, 1–2 hours
Elevation Gain: 1,700'
Difficulty: Beginner, Moderate
Map: p. 89

Notes: Although a paved road ride, Thompson Creek Road is sufficiently out of the way to be a real country ride. With the initial climb, you'll be glad to have that low gear range. Jerome Park, the high, wide valley at the top of the ride where the Spring Gulch cross-country center operates in the winter time, is the eastern end of the Colorado Plateau, the vast highlands that includes Colorado's western slope and all of Utah's canyon country. The steeply tilted sedimentary rocks to the east of the park were pushed up by the igneous rock that formed Mount Sopris at the western edge of the Rocky Mountains. As you ride up the long hill, you can see and feel the change from the upthrusting mountains to the interior west of canyons and cowboy movies.

Access: At the Carbondale Main Street stoplight on Highway 133, go west on the Main Street extension (County Road 108).

Route: A ¼-mile stretch leads to the Crystal River where the road curves right to follow the east bank for ½ mile to the Colorado Rocky Mountain School. Here the road curves left and drops to cross the river. Almost immediately it begins the steep ¼-mile climb up Sweet Hill to a 1 ½-mile wide bench occupied by a ranch with gorgeous views of Mount Sopris. After the bench the road begins the moderate 3-mile long climb up to Jerome Park. One mile up the hill, on the right, is Dry Park Road (County Road 125), an enjoyable back way to Glenwood Springs (see Route #50). The climb eases as the road bends south into Jerome Park; the logical turnaround is at the Spring Gulch ski trails 1 ½ miles on. One-half mile past the ski area the Forest Service Thompson Creek Road forks left down the hill, the beginning of the Tall Pines route (see Route #51).

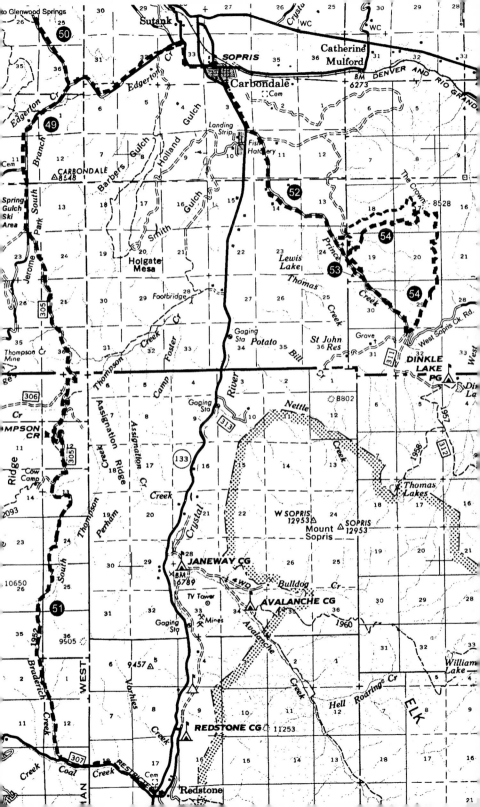

50. Dry Park Road

One Way: 5 ¾ miles, ½ –1 hour
Elevation Gain: (from Carbondale) minimal/ (from Glenwood) 600'
Difficulty: Beginner/Intermediate, Moderate
Map: p. 89

Notes: A sign at the beginning of the road reads "Impassable when wet" and it means what it says; the deep ruts frequently driven into the red clay in the middle section of the road are the only technical difficulties you might encounter. Dry Park is similar to Jerome Park—a high bench valley between ridges formed by harder layers of sedimentary rock. The riding is standard dirt road; the views back to Sopris and across the Roaring Fork Valley to Basalt and Red Table mountains, the Flat Tops, and Glenwood Canyon put you on another plane. If you're looking for an out-of-the-way moderate ride, you can do it on its own. Mostly, Dry Park Road is used as a fun way to get from Carbondale to Glenwood.

Dry Park Road—the homestretch of an Aspen-to-Glenwood ride.

Access: From the stoplight intersection of Main Street and Highway 133 in Carbondale, take the Thompson Creek Road route (see Route #49) 3.8 miles to its junction with Dry Park Road (County Road 125), a gravel road that starts out across a cattle guard on the right.

Route: The first mile starts out level or gently climbing through piñon/juniper forest and grassland, then begins descending with views across ranchland into the Flat Tops. The second mile brings you to a ranch house; another mile of rocky road through the hayfields leads to a steep descent through scrub oak and piñon—the part of the road you don't want to ride when wet. After ½ mile the road levels out again, then rolls along for another 1 ½ miles through the dry country forest to the next ranch and the first view up Glenwood Canyon. Three-quarters mile further on the road ends at Four Mile Road; turn right for the fast, 4-mile run into Glenwood, or left for the long climb up to Ski Sunlight and Four Mile Park (see Route #64).

51. Tall Pines (So. Thompson & Braderich Cr.)

One Way: 17 ½ miles, 3–5 hours
Elevation Gain: 2,700'
Difficulty: Advanced, Strenuous
Map: p. 89

Notes: A classic cross-country route, over-hill-and-down-dale from Carbondale to Redstone. The surface goes from graded road through smooth double track to rough single track, with a short paved descent at the end. This is a disastrous route to attempt when it's muddy; 4-wheel drive trucks with chains can't get safely through the first section, and the final single-track descent can be a quagmire.

Access: (See Route #49). One-half mile past the Spring Gulch ski touring center fork left onto Forest Road 305, 7.5 miles from Highway 133 in Carbondale. There is plenty of informal parking at this junction.

Route: The ride begins with a fast, fairly smooth 2 ½-mile descent from Jerome Park to North Thompson Creek. Cross the creek and climb moderately to a saddle at the eastern end of Stony Ridge with views south along Lake Ridge (where you're headed) and northeast to the vertical sandstone fins on the other side of North Thompson Creek. Another smooth, winding mile (pass the South Branch Road, Forest Road 306, at .4 miles on the right) brings you to Willow Park on Middle Thompson Creek. Bear left across a bridge and begin climbing moderately for nearly a mile up a long narrow draw that opens up into a broad, meadowy swale. The road switchbacks up the side of the oak-covered ridge to the east; the pitch eases off as it traverses in and out of a long gully and onto the top of the ridge. The road runs straight along the ridge to its crest (a close-up view of Mount Sopris and up Avalanche Creek to Capitol Peak), then bears right and down to a saddle.

Climb west from the saddle for ¼ mile, bear left onto a rough 4-wheel drive track just before a gate on the main road. The track sidehills down to a creek bed, climbs the other side steeply and repeats the process in the next gully before emerging onto a ridgetop and descending easterly into a meadow. It fades a bit here but becomes clearer as it starts up the hill on the other side for a ½-mile climb that curves westward onto the sage-covered top of the next ridge, known as Parsnip Flat. Three fences converge on the crest of the ridge; bear left through a gate and follow the marked South Thompson Creek Trail (Trail 1952) along the left side of the middle fence. The trail descends gradually through the oak brush and across a meadow, then drops steeply to a creek crossing. Climb out of the creek and bear right through a meadow, go through a fence, then a

gate, and leave the road to follow a single track along the fence until it merges with the road again. The road gradually deteriorates into a single track as you descend a sidehill to yet another creek crossing—the price of traveling across the grain of the land. Push or carry your bike a good 200 yards up the steep climb on the other side to get to the heart of the ride—2 ¼ miles of varied single tracking through aspen groves and meadows, in and out of more gullies, to the top of the pass, visible as the tree-covered saddle to the south.

Beaver sign along the Tall Pines trail.

A heavy snake fence of aspen logs marks the summit, and handsome old aspen trees converge on the meadow that opens up on the south side—a fine place for a well-earned break. From the summit descend along the west side of the drainage into the woods for some tricky riding and a long sidehill to the main creek crossing, a mile below the summit. From here you get good views across Coal Basin to the south end of Lake Ridge—behind you now. Cross another creek and bear right down through the meadow parallel to the creek. From here on down the trail is roughed up and sometimes braided from heavy livestock traffic. Just before the end the trail climbs a short pitch to the left and then drops down some very steep switchbacks to a left onto the paved road (Forest Road 307) and a fast 2 ½ miles to Highway 133 and the Crystal River. Turn upstream for .1 mile and cross the bridge to Redstone for some civilized refreshment. From Redstone it's 17 miles—an hour or less of fast downstream cruising—back to Carbondale on Highway 133.

52. Prince Creek Road

Round Trip: (from Carbondale) 15 miles, 1–2 hours
Elevation Gain: 2,000'
Difficulty: Beginner, Moderate
Map: p. 89

Notes: Prince Creek Road is the closest dirt riding to Carbondale—a quick escape from the street grid and the Worldwide Web—and the access route to several other rides: Porcupine Loop (Route #53), Crown Trails (Route #54), West Sopris Creek (Route #37), Hay Park (Route #38). It starts out in the biggest patch of ranchland left in the Roaring Fork Valley and climbs up through the gambel oak forest to the beginning of the aspen zone.

Access: From Carbondale, pick up Highway 133 south toward Redstone; 1 ½ miles from the center of Carbondale, where the residential development gives way to ranches, Prince Creek Road starts off to the left.

Route: The road heads east for ¼ mile, then turns south parallel to Highway 133 for a mile, with a clear view of the north gully of Mount Sopris straight ahead. By a red barn, the road bears left and begins following the creek with mixed easy climbing and level stretches. The pavement lasts for another 1 ¼ miles; once the road turns to dirt the climbing becomes steadier. Two miles further up, the road leaves the creek and begins a moderately steep climb up a dusty (or very muddy) cut in the side of the hill, which lasts the final 1 ½ miles to the top of the divide, with a brief break just below the top. At the divide the right fork leads up the ridge to Dinkle Lake (see Route #37) and Hay Park Trail (Route #38), the left fork goes over the divide to West Sopris Creek Road and, just over the top, to the start of the Crown Trails (see Route #54).

53. Porcupine Loop

Round Trip: (from Carbondale) 13 miles, 1–2 hours
Elevation Gain: 1,100'
Difficulty: Intermediate, Easy
Maps: pp. 89, 95

Notes: This loop is a quick, fun ride readily accessible from downtown with pastoral views across the lower Roaring Fork Valley. Essentially a variant of the Prince Creek Road (Route #52), Porcupine Loop adds a flying, banking cruise along an old water ditch to an otherwise unexceptional route.

Access: (See Route #52). At 4 ¼ miles up Prince Creek Road (1 ½ miles past the end of the pavement, across from some campsites by the creek) a dirt road diverges sharply back to the left.

Route: Follow the dirt road as it winds around the base of the hill for ½ mile; at the start of a left-hand hairpin turn up a short hill, make a sharper left onto a single track (if you keep going on the road you'll eventually climb all the way up onto the Crown). This is the "ditch", which winds into gullies and around ridges for an all-too-brief 1 ¼ miles, then ends at a 4-wheel drive road (which also comes down from the Crown). Turn sharply left onto this road for a quick, loose descent back to Prince Creek Road ¾ mile below where you left it.

54. Crown Trails

Round Trip: 8 ½ –9 miles, 1–2 hours
Elevation Gain: 1,900'
Difficulty: Intermediate, Strenuous
Maps: pp. 89, 95

Notes: A rocking and rolling little loop close to Carbondale and El Jebel, Crown Trails is a mid-altitude (8882' peak) ride with mostly southern exposure, no dark timber, and well-drained soil, so it's good in the early and late seasons when many rides are mudded out. And it's still 2,500'

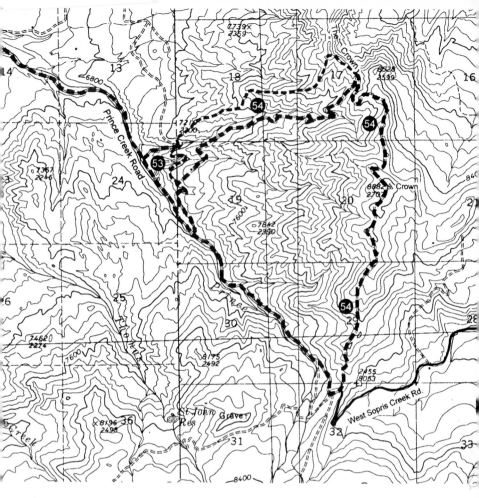

above the valley floor so you get some great views and the feeling of being up there.

Access: The ride starts on the divide near the junction of the Prince Creek Road (see Route #52) and West Sopris Creek Road (see Route #37), so you can approach it from either Carbondale or Basalt. One-tenth mile east (West Sopris Creek side) of the junction, go north through a parking area and straight up a steep 4-wheel drive track.

Route: The first climb is a ¼-mile push—the ride really begins on top of the first knoll. Roll along the ridge for ¼ mile to the start of a ½-mile climb, which is a grunt but very doable. This ends the heavy work; from here cruise along the ridge ½ mile to the second summit, then down and up to the height of land and a 360-degree panorama that takes in (from the west) Assignation Ridge, Sunlight, the Flat Tops, Red Table, Basalt Mountain, Williams Mountains, New York Peak, Snowmass Ski Area,

Sopris and the Prince Creek Divide from the Crown route.

Capitol Peak, and last and most prominent, Mount Sopris. A little past the summit the road drops steeply and then rolls along the ragged crest of the ridge to a major fork in the road 1 ¼ miles from the summit. Take the left fork and begin the winding, 3-mile descent back into the valley. At the bottom of the hill the road levels and follows a water ditch ½ mile south to Prince Creek Road. From here it's a moderate 2-mile, 900' climb back to the divide.

To extend the ride a little and take in a more challenging descent, follow the left fork (referred to above) for ½ mile, then go right on a short connecting road that takes you back up to a saddle on the ridge (the road that follows the ridge down to this saddle gets too steep and rutted out to ride safely). Go left and climb ¼ mile to the next summit (the top of the steep headwall known as The Crown), then turn left again onto a faint, rough track that descends steeply along a ridge line down to the ditch. Turn left along the ditch for a mile of fast, winding single track back to rejoin the regular descent route out to Prince Creek Road.

55. Schofield Pass Road to Crested Butte

One Way: (to Crested Butte) 23 miles, 3–5 hours
Round Trip: (to Schofield Pass and back) 19 miles, 3–5 hours
Elevation Gain: 2,400'/2,300'
Difficulty: Intermediate/Advanced, Moderate
Map: p. 98

Notes: Schofield Pass (10,707') is the lowest, easiest pass between the Roaring Fork Valley and Crested Butte. Making an overnight trip of it is a good introduction to mountain bike touring, and the canyon and river scenery give little away to the alpine spectacle of the higher passes. Excepting the two miles east of Crystal, the going is easy to moderate with only a few miles of rocky road. From the top of the pass into Crested Butte it's smooth and fast, with the last several miles paved.

Access: Take Highway 133 south from Carbondale 22 miles to the Marble turnoff on the left at the base of McClure Pass. Drive 6 miles south on this road to Marble, keep going another 2 miles through town, past Beaver Lake, and up to the top of Daniels Hill and the junction of the Crystal and Lost Trail Creek (Lead King Basin) roads. Even on the busiest weekend you should be able to find a place to park near here. One can start from Marble but that just adds the long, steep, uninteresting climb up Daniels Hill to the ride.

A rainy descent through Devil's Punchbowl, Schofield Pass Road.

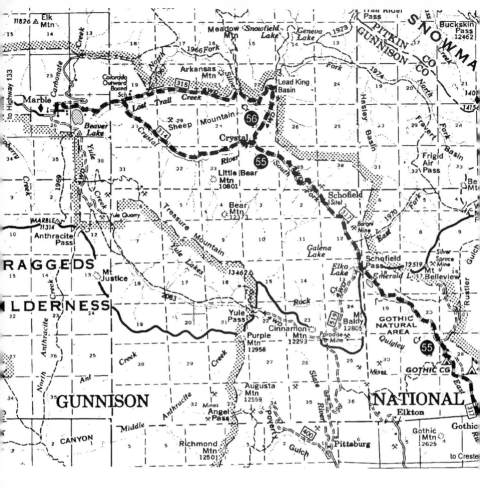

Route: From the top of Daniels Hill drop down a narrow shelf road and cross a bridge to Lizard Lake, a shallow pond perched improbably on the edge of a canyon. Pass around the west side of the lake and drop down again to the Crystal River. The road hugs the river for the most part, with a couple of short, rough climbs to get over riverside ledges. The first mile or so is pretty rocky, then the road smooths out—though it always seems to be full of puddles. Three miles up the avalanche-scoured canyon is the much-photographed Crystal Mill (also known as the Dead Horse Mill) resting on a ledge above a small waterfall. One-quarter mile past the mill is the Crystal town site—a handful of old cabins with a few inhabitants on either side of a very rocky "main street." One-quarter mile on the other side of town turn left up a hill at the "End of Maintained Road" sign. The climb begins benignly enough but then switches back to the right for a ¾-mile loose, rocky climb with the turnoff to Lead King Basin (on the left; see Route #56) about halfway up. The road levels off briefly, then comes the ¾-mile push up through the aptly named Devil's Punchbowl, a dark, crumbling canyon with the road clinging to a shelf blasted out of its southern side.

Coming out of the Punchbowl is like coming out of Purgatory—the road levels off and fords the river into an open, wooded valley. After a level one-half mile, a short climb past a waterfall leads to the old Schofield town site at the lower end of Schofield Park and views of the high, colorful ridges to the north. The park goes on for 1 ½ miles; at the south end the road crosses the river once more and begins a moderate ¾-mile climb to the top of the pass—a level spot at 10,700 feet in the middle of the woods.

The road breaks out of the woods and traverses down a steep slope above Emerald Lake to follow the meandering East River into Gothic, a bit larger than Crystal and now the home of the Rocky Mountain

Biological Laboratory—a world-renowned research center humbly housed in restored miners' cabins. One-half mile past Gothic the road crosses the river and begins a 3-mile traverse up across the north face of Snodgrass Mountain to the divide just above the Crested Butte Ski Area. Here the road reverts to pavement for the last, fast few miles through Mt. Crested Butte into the town of Crested Butte.

Main Street, Crystal City, Colorado (no zip code).

56. Lead King Basin/Lost Trail Creek

Round Trip: 12 ½ miles, 3–5 hours
Elevation Gain: 2,500'
Difficulty: Advanced, Strenuous
Map: p. 98

Notes: In my estimation, this is the most beautiful ride in this book. Lead King Basin, at the heart of this route, is one of the most unusual alpine valleys in the area—a lush, grassy opening among the craggy peaks created by glaciers converging from three sides. The route is all 4-wheel drive roads, but of the sort where people regularly manage to roll their vehicles, so there's a good dose of rock-hopping mixed in with riding that demands no more than picking a smooth line through the rocks and ruts. The first 5 miles through Crystal to Lead King Basin are the rough and rocky part of the ride, the return leg is mostly smooth—though hardly level and even—dirt.

Access: (See Route #55). The best place to park is at or just before the top of Daniels Hill where the Crystal and Lost Trail Creek roads meet. The road just past the top of the hill is a narrow ledge with only one small turnout, so even a little traffic gets very complicated.

Route: The route rides counterclockwise; at the top of Daniels Hill take the right fork to Crystal City. Drop down the narrow ledge road to a bridge, then wind through the bushes to Lizard Lake—an improbable pond sitting in a saddle with sheer cliffs behind it and a deep valley to either side. Just past the lake the road drops down along another narrow shelf to the Crystal River, a rocky mountain stream running beneath the steep, avalanche-scoured slopes of Treasure Mountain. With the exception of a couple of short, steep climbs the road up the Crystal River is 3 miles of rocky but enjoyable riding with a few smooth, shady interludes where the forest has grown up between the avalanche paths. Just before the Crystal town site is the much-photographed Crystal Mill—a narrow barn sitting on a rocky point above the creek with a square tower of stacked wooden beams reaching down into the water. Crystal itself is an all but ghost town with a "General Store" offering souvenirs and candy bars on an irregular schedule.

Two hundred yards beyond Crystal the road turns sharply left up a hill and maintenance, such as it is, ceases. At first this makes little difference, but then the road switches back to the right and the next few hundred yards up to the Lead King Basin turnoff are a rock pile that will test anyone's stamina and skill. The turnoff (to the left) provides some relief from the climbing, though the surface continues to be loose and rocky for another one-third mile until the road passes through the gate of high cliffs that flank the entrance to the valley. As the valley opens up the views become progressively more spectacular and the road easier to ride. For a while it goes back into the woods for some fun twisting and turning with a few tricky rock steps, then suddenly comes out of the trees into Lead King Basin, 1 ½ miles from the turnoff.

At the entrance to the basin the road forks; take the left fork across a bridge and begin climbing up along the other side of the creek. The climb up to the Lost Trail divide is long (2 ¾ miles) but not overly steep (1,300' elevation gain). It starts out switching back and forth through the

The gateway to Lead King Basin.

aspen, then breaks out into wildflower meadows with views of the backsides of Snowmass Mountain and the Maroon Bells and the twisted rock layers of Bear Basin across the Crystal River. Once the switchbacks are over the climb becomes an easy traverse until the road makes a sharp left turn and suddenly you're descending—a 4-mile swooping, hollering descent down dusty, rutty switchbacks and through the woods—back to the starting point.

57. Ragged Mountain Trail

One Way: 19 ½ miles, 4–6 hours
Elevation Gain: 2,600'
Difficulty: Advanced, Strenuous
Map: p. 103

Notes: The Ragged Mountain Trail is a classic trail ride through one corner of the world's largest aspen forest. Only ½ mile of it is in the Roaring Fork watershed, but with 15 miles of very ridable single and double track it's too good to leave out of this book. Overall, the ride loses 2,000' of altitude—which makes for a lot of good cruising and long descents—but there are enough ups to go with the downs to make you wonder when they will ever end. It's definitely not an out-and-back ride, so you need to set up a shuttle.

Access: Take Highway 133 south from Carbondale to top of McClure Pass (26 miles). Park on the south side of the highway in a large gravel lot. At east end of lot is a gate and the start of Forest Service Road 898. To set up the shuttle, drive 19 miles down the west side of McClure Pass to the Kebler Pass Road (County Road 12) just below the Paonia Reservoir Dam. Drive 6 miles up the Kebler Pass Road and park at the Erickson Springs Campground, just across Anthracite Creek and before the road begins climbing out of the valley.

Route: From the parking lot take Road 898, which traverses along the Crystal River side of the ridge and then crosses over to the Muddy Creek side, drops briefly, and begins the long, easy climb to the trailhead (2 ¾ miles from Highway 133). The road traverses southwest for a little over a mile, then doglegs south for ½ mile, and curves back to the north around a knoll to the trailhead just before a locked gate. You can also park here on the left side of the road; the trail drops off on the right side.

After a short descent, the trail begins contouring around to the south, out of the aspen and into the spruce/fir forest as the trail climbs moderately

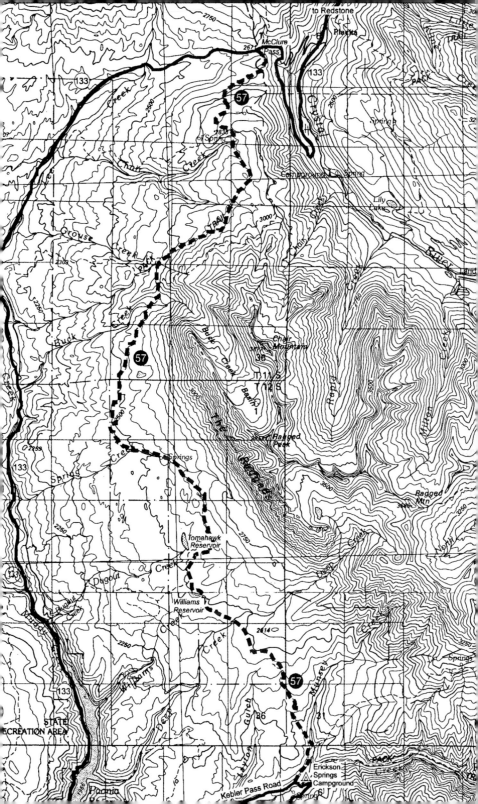

for 1 mile up to the head of Chair Creek. Crossing over a ridge, the trail begins an easy descent for 1 ½ miles through the forest and across several small streams to emerge in a rocky meadow with long views out to the west. Just the other side of the meadow, the trail joins a private road. Follow the orange diamonds on the trees (snowmobile route markers) as the road continues descending for another mile to an intersection—there are several homesites being developed in this relatively level area. Start climbing steeply up the left fork through the aspen groves to a T-intersection on a ridgetop with spectacular views along the Raggeds ridge and up into Buck Creek Basin between the Raggeds and Chair Mountain. Most of the remainder of the ride will be along the base of the Raggeds, with the views improving as you go along.

Cross the road and begin a traversing descent on a single track that becomes increasingly steep and technical toward the bottom. At the bottom of the hill turn right onto a double track for ¼ mile, then bear left across another double track onto a single track. Cross Buck Creek and push up a steep hill to be rewarded with several miles of gorgeous riding through the aspen groves and the first glimpses of the Raggeds—a rocky, buttressed ridge shredded with gullies. Two miles along is another short push up along a fence line, then descend two-thirds mile into a meadow. Turn left in the center of the meadow onto an offroad vehicle-sized double track which climbs back up into the aspen forest. One-half mile along a trail crosses the double track and the creek on the right—keep going straight on the double track and around the spring that's the source of the creek. The trail continues its enjoyable climb through the aspen for another 1 ½ miles—mostly easy with a few short, technical rocky pitches to keep your heart beating. From this high point the trail makes another long, lovely 2-mile descent with few obstacles to the Williams Creek Reservoir. Ride or walk out onto the dam for a great view of Marcellina Mountain and the West Elks.

From the reservoir, the trail climbs east toward Ragged Mountain, then drops down to Deep Creek, and up the final ½-mile climb. The last descent is the longest—first 1 ½ miles down a sometimes steep and loose double track, then 1 ½ miles down Mumsey Creek Road to the Kebler Pass Road just across the creek from the campground.

Glenwood Springs

There are excellent rides in the Glenwood Springs area for all levels of ability and ambition, ranging from the concrete bike path along Interstate 70 through Glenwood Canyon to endless miles of challenging jeep trails in the Flat Tops. The city of Glenwood Springs is also developing a system of paved bike paths along the Roaring Fork and Colorado rivers in town; this is an ongoing process with the system expanding year by year. The hub of this system is Two Rivers Park between the Interstate and the north bank of the Colorado River. Designed primarily for local traffic and the casual tourist around town, it will also serve riders interested in getting to the rides described in this book without becoming part of the downtown traffic jam.

All of the rides described below can be reached from Two Rivers Park or downtown Glenwood, and for most of them it makes sense to start here. To reach Two Rivers Park from downtown, go north across the Grand Avenue Bridge, turn left onto 6th Street, go .2 miles through the light and past the Ramada Inn to a left turn onto Devereux Road, go over the Interstate, down a short hill, and left into the parking area. From the I-70 exit, turn left at the first light onto 6th Street and left again onto Devereux Road.

58. Glenwood Canyon Bike Path

Round Trip: 31 miles, 2–4 hours
Elevation Gain: 600'
Difficulty: Beginner, Easy
Map: p. 108 (only beginning of trail shown on map)

Notes: A lot of reward for not much effort, Glenwood Canyon is one of the most spectacular landforms around and the best way to see it is from the bike path. I-70 is always present—as often as not as a concrete retaining wall next to your shoulder—but the towering rock walls and the Colorado River easily overshadow it. You don't have to be in great shape or much of a rider to tackle this bike path, but it's also a great place for strong riders to get in some quality spinning time while enjoying Nature's landscaping at its best. The principal drawback is all the other people enjoying it along with you, particularly around the rest areas, though the crowd thins out toward the eastern end and you can go for miles without encountering anyone.

Sneaking under I-70 along the Colorado River, Glenwood Canyon Bike Path.

Access: (from Glenwood Springs) Go right (east) on 6th street at the north end of the Grand Avenue Bridge; the bike path begins just beyond the vapor caves spa. There is plenty of parking in the area around the hot springs pool. (from Dotsero) You can also get onto the bike path at the eastern end; immediately north of the Dotsero exit on I-70 is a frontage road that runs 2 miles back along the highway to a parking area at the start of the bike path.

Route: Ride along the interstate on old US 6 pavement for nearly a mile, then cross I-70 on a pedestrian bridge and drop down to the old road again as it swings out around Horseshoe Bend. At the other end of the bend the old road becomes the main street of No Name, Colorado. Climb up a ½-mile hill (the longest on the bike path) to the crest; the bike path drops down to the right to meet the river again. There's a rest area at the top of the hill, the next one is another 2 ½ miles at Grizzly Creek, where most of the Colorado River raft trips are launched. Between No Name and Grizzly the path is quite flat and swings away from the highway for a bit, adding to the peacefulness of the ride.

The path through Grizzly is quite convoluted and crowded, take it slowly. Beyond Grizzly the path begins to climb a little to the Shoshone put-in and the power plant 1 ½ miles upriver. Between Shoshone and the dam is the narrowest part of the canyon; the path is a fenced-in ramp between the rocks of the riverbed and the wall of the highway. Two miles above Shoshone the path begins a ½-mile climb up to the top of the dam and the Hanging Lake Rest Area, 9 ½ miles from the start. One-half mile further on is the Hanging Lake Trailhead, a peaceful spot in the heart of the canyon and a good place to make your turnaround if you're not interested in gong the whole way.

Beyond Hanging Lake the path levels out again for the 5 ½ miles to its end. There's one more rest stop at Bair Ranch, 3 miles along. This part of the canyon isn't quite as spectacular as the lower section, but the quiet water behind the dam and a little more space around the highway makes for a much more intimate experience of the river and its canyon. Be prepared for strong headwinds on the return trip—they can make the run downriver as time-consuming and almost as much work as the ride up.

59. Red Mountain Road

Round Trip: (from 8th Street Bridge) 6 miles, 1–2 hours
Elevation Gain: 1,600′
Difficulty: Intermediate, Strenuous
Map: p. 108

Notes: Glenwood Springs once had an in-town ski area. Red Mountain Road served as its access road; you can still see traces of ski trails and a few tow frames. Now it's an in-town bike run—a good moderate climb ending at a spectacular viewpoint overlooking the town and the Roaring Fork Valley up to Mount Sopris, followed by a fast, sometimes bumpy descent with lots of hairpin turns. A new water plant is being built on top of part of the road, so for now the bottom ¼ mile is a steep single track—push up and ride down if you dare.

Access: (from Two Rivers Park) Cross the Colorado River, turn right across 8th Street Bridge to Midland Avenue. (from Grand Avenue) Turn west on 8th Street, ride two blocks to Pitkin Avenue, turn right for one block to 7th Street, left on 7th to 8th Street Bridge.

Route: At the west end of the 8th Street Bridge, turn right onto Midland Avenue, curve left onto Red Mountain Drive to 9th Street which goes right up a steep hill and becomes Red Mountain Road. The gravel road curves right after 100 yards, go straight ahead and follow single track which climbs steeply up the left side of the gulch. Regain gravel road for 2 ¾ miles of steady, gentle to moderate climbing to the lookout. At the top, keep to the left, several private roads diverge to the right.

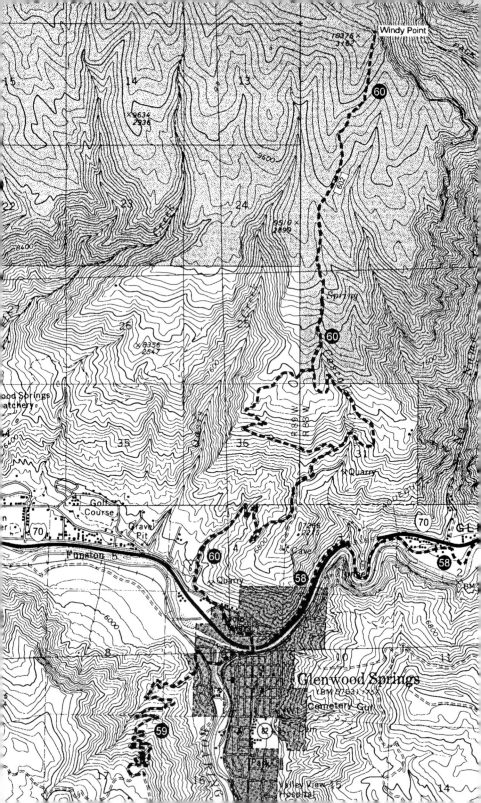

Glenwood Springs and the lower Roaring Fork Valley from Red Mountain.

60. Transfer Trail

Round Trip: [Loop] (from upper parking area) 5 ¼ miles, 1–2 hours
(from lower parking area) 9 ½ miles, 2–3 hours;
[Windy Point] 11 ½ miles, 3–4 hours / 15 ½ miles, 4–6 hours
Elevation Gain: [Loop] 1,400'/2,500'; [Windy Point] 3,400'/4,500'
Difficulty: Advanced, Strenuous
Map: p. 108

Notes: Get ready for a wild ride on the edge of the canyon—no fearful drops but plenty of dramatic views. Transfer Trail is a good climbing route easily accessible from downtown Glenwood that has several parts and possibilities—the lower gravel road makes for a quick, hard workout; the upper loop provides more strenuous fun and takes you up out of the valley and onto the rim of the Flat Tops. From there you can continue on the strenuous, 2,000' climb up to Windy Point above No Name Canyon. Heart-stopping views up the Roaring Fork Valley make it easy to understand the Utes' reverence for Mount Sopris.

Access: Go west on 6th Street/Route 6 from the Grand Avenue Bridge; ¼ mile west of the Ramada Inn turn right onto Traver Trail Road. Four-tenths mile up Traver Trail Road, turn right onto a gravel road on the outside of a left-hand hairpin turn. There is a sign and some parking at this roadhead.

Route: A roughly graded road with loose gravel on the surface heads up a dry creek drainage for ¾ mile before switching back up the ridge to the east. One-half mile further on is a short level stretch, then the road climbs another ½ mile to a large graveled parking area on a neck of land overlooking quarries on either side. You can easily drive to this point to ride the upper, more interesting, section.

Head north out of parking area across the narrow point of neck, slab right up across the side of the canyon toward the next ridge to east, which overlooks No Name Creek. One-half mile up the road splits, the left fork is the return end of the loop. It could be ridden either way, but the west side is considerably rockier and rougher and would be an expert level challenge to climb. Take the right fork which continues around to the far side of the gulch, then switches back onto the ridge—getting up around the turn without dabbing is a challenge. The next ¾ mile up the ridge offers a number of strenuous, somewhat technical climbing sections. After climbing up a little draw, the road switches back to the west again and emerges above the rim of the canyon for a spectacular view up the Roaring Fork River and Four Mile Creek. The road heads north again from the overlook to a fork ¼ mile back in the woods. Windy Point is 3 rough miles straight ahead on Forest Road 602; bear left to finish the loop. Soon after the fork, the road crests the ridge and begins its 2 ¼ mile descent to the end of the loop.

61. Red Canyon Road

Round Trip: 12 miles, 1 ½–3 hours
Elevation Gain: 1,100'
Difficulty: Beginner, Moderate
Map: p. 111

Notes: Red Canyon Road is a good, moderate ride that combines a climb up a pretty little canyon through piñon covered hills with a cruise across the wide-open farmland of Spring Valley with its panoramic views of the mountains to the south and west. This route is also used as the access road to Lookout Mountain Road (see Route #62) and the Boy Scout Trail (see Route #63). You can park at the mouth of the canyon or ride out from downtown Glenwood Springs.

Access: Red Canyon Road (County Road 115) leaves Highway 82 at the 3.8-mile point, just south of the Buffalo Valley Restaurant. Turn off to the east side of the highway and bear 45 degrees right up the hill. There is a parking turnout at the hairpin curve ¼ mile up the hill. To ride from

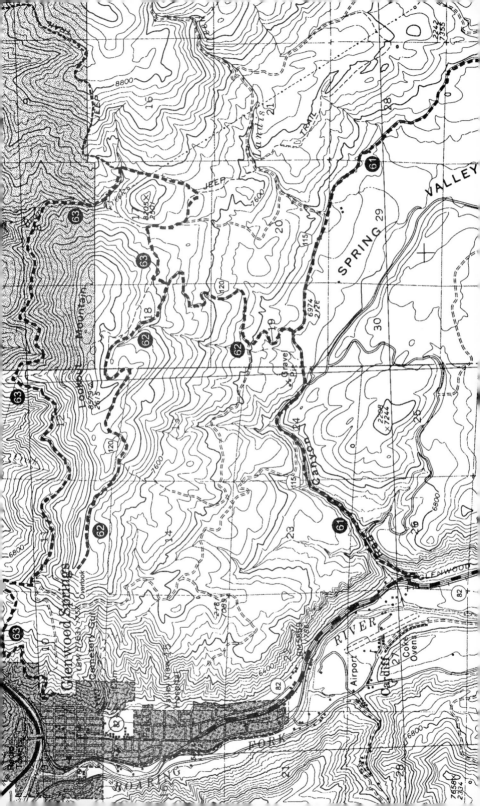

Glenwood Springs, take Pitkin Avenue (2 blocks west of Grand Avenue) south to 14th Street, turn right onto Roaring Fork Drive, circle around the High School campus to Park Drive, follow it back out to Grand Avenue. Ride the sidewalk along Grand to 23rd Street where Highway 82 verges left—stay right on South Grand Avenue and follow it all the way to its end at Highway 82, a few hundred yards shy of Red Canyon Road on the opposite side.

Route: After rounding the hairpin curve at the beginning, the Red Canyon Road clings to a narrow shelf on the south wall of the red rock canyon. At ¾ mile the rock walls end and the road winds along the stream course through the piñon forest for 2 miles; a last steep pitch brings you out into Spring Valley with its open ranchland flanked by oak-covered hills. Four-tenths mile past the exit from the canyon, County Road 120 to Lookout Mountain (see Route #62), the Boy Scout Trail (see Route #63), and Hubbard Cave takes off up the hill to the left. From here Red Canyon Road rolls along the east side of Spring Valley to its junction with Spring Valley Road (County Road 114; see Route #43).

62. Lookout Mountain Road

Round Trip: (from Red Canyon Rd.) 11 miles, 2–3 hours/
(from Hwy. 82) 17 miles, 3–4 hours
Elevation Gain: 1,700'/2,700'
Difficulty: Intermediate, Moderate
Map: p. 111

Notes: Lookout Mountain Road (County Road 120) turns the trip up Red Canyon into something more than an evening cruise. And at the end of the road you're looking straight down into both Glenwood Canyon and the Roaring Fork Valley. Hang gliders have been known to use it as a launch site.

Access: (See Route #61). Follow Red Canyon Road as described in Route #61 through the canyon to .4 miles past the exit from the canyon where County Road 120 to Lookout Mountain takes off up the hill to the left.

Route: Lookout Mountain Road switchbacks up from Red Canyon Road into the scrub oak at a moderate pitch with some loose gravel and washboard; the view extends all the way from Sunlight Peak to Aspen Mountain and into the Sawatch Range. One and two-thirds miles up is a parking area on the right for Hubbard Cave and the Boy Scout Trail (see

Route #63). (Lookout Mountain Road loops around to the west and comes back; ½ mile above the parking area a 4-wheel drive cutoff on the right also connects to the Boy Scout Trail route.) At 3 miles the climb eases off and contours around a draw and out to the ridge line again. From here the road actually descends 300' over the last 2 miles to the overlook with views of the Roaring Fork Valley and Storm King Mountain along the way.

63. Boy Scout Trail

One Way: (from Red Canyon Road) 12 miles, 3–5 hours
Elevation Gain: 1,000'
Difficulty: Advanced/Expert, Moderate
Map: p. 111

Notes: The ride known as the "Boy Scout Trail" (only the end of which is actually on the Boy Scout Trail up Lookout Mountain) is a unique ride in this area—5 miles of single track traversing along the side of Glenwood Canyon, followed by a wild and wonderful descent right into Glenwood Springs. Anyone not comfortable with sidehill riding will either get comfortable (it's not terribly difficult) or have a miserable time. The final descent is the most technical part.

Access: Take Red Canyon Road (County Road 115) east from Highway 82 (at 3.8-mile point near Buffalo Valley Restaurant just south of Glenwood Springs) 3 miles to County Road 120, on the left. If you're doing a shuttle, drive 1.7 miles up Road 120 and park in the large graveled lot on the right.

Route: Exit at the rear of the parking lot on a jeep road that bears right. The road climbs through the brush; at .4 miles a left fork goes back to Road 120. Keep right, pass through a gate and down a hill past a pasture with a view across to the north rim of Glenwood Canyon. Keep heading eastward across rolling terrain toward a power line for another ¾ mile. The road veers left and climbs to the power line, then begins descending with a full view across the canyon. About ¼ mile down, at the bottom of the descent, turn left onto a double track down Bear Gulch. (The main road goes up a hill and on to Hubbard Cave, a 6-mile out-and-back ride with about 1,100' of steep climbing and descending and great views of the canyon.) Three-quarters mile down through the aspen trees, the Boy Scout Trail forks left, 100' past an old earthen dam. It's a narrow single track and easy to miss because of deadfall in front of the sign. If you come to a creek crossing, turn around and go back.

The trail begins with some tricky sidehill riding as it works its way out of the gulch and onto the side of the canyon where the riding becomes a little easier. It winds through the conifer forest on an almost dead-level traverse—cool, pleasant riding but with few views of the canyon. At 2 ½ miles out the trail comes out to a point where the forest changes to scrub oak and you can finally see down the main canyon and across the river to No Name Creek. The Lookout Mountain Trail (hiking) climbs up the ridge on the left. From here on the trail platform widens to wagon road width, allowing for faster and less risky riding with almost continuous views. However, there is still lots of body contact with the brush—the easily-scratched should consider wearing tights and long sleeves. All along you need to keep your sunglasses on, even in the shade—you take a lot of twigs in the face, with deadfall and low branches to duck under. After another 2 ½ miles you round a corner to views of the Roaring Fork Valley and Red Mountain on the west side of Glenwood. One-tenth mile past the corner the upper part of the Boy Scout hiking trail diverges uphill

toward the radio towers—stay on the road for another one-tenth mile and then plunge right onto a steep, eroded single track (the lower part of the Boy Scout hiking trail). The trail levels out for a delightful, winding descent along the crest of a ridge and then becomes very steep and loose as it drops off the end of the ridge. Again it eases off for 2 miles of smooth, rolling switchbacks all the way to the upper end of 8th Street, 3 blocks from the heart of Glenwood Springs.

Shady riding on the Boy Scout Trail.

64. Four Mile Park Road

Round Trip: 26 miles, 3–5 hours/(from Glenwood) 46 miles, 5–7 hours
Elevation Gain: 3,100'/5,500'
Difficulty: Beginner, Moderate
Map: p. 116

Notes: A long, moderate ride out into the hills and open parks west of Glenwood Springs, Four Mile Park Road (Forest Road 300) begins near the Sunlight Ski Area. Bring your topographic maps and explore some of the many roads and trails that branch off from Road 300; it also connects with roads to Silt, Colbran, Paonia, and points west for real cross-country riding.

Access: From the junction of Grand Avenue and Highway 82 in Glenwood Springs (23rd Street), take South Grand Avenue along the river to the 27th Street (Sunlight) Bridge. Cross the bridge and turn left onto Midland Avenue, fork right onto Four Mile Road (County Road 117) 1 ¼ miles south of the bridge. The county road climbs in a series of short steep pitches broken by long easy stretches for 3 miles to the junction with Dry Park Road (see Route #50). From here it climbs steadily and easily for 5 ½ miles up a pleasant stream valley to the start of Four Mile Park Road (Forest Road 300) on the right. If you're riding from downtown Glenwood, you might want to take the 8th Street Bridge to Midland Avenue to avoid the Grand Avenue traffic altogether.

Route: Road 300 traverses gently up along the south slope of Sunlight Peak, winding in and out of gulches, in and out of aspen groves with views across to the Sunlight Ski Area on the other side of the valley. Two miles further, Forest Road 318 to the top of Sunlight Peak (see Route #65) forks off to the right. Road 300 then crosses the creek (there's a good parking area just on the other side) and makes a steep switchback turn to begin traversing up around the base of Williams Peak. A second 2 miles brings you to Four Mile Park where the road turns south and levels out for ½ mile before beginning its major climb—3 miles past beaver ponds, up through the aspen forest into the spruce/fir, through an old clearcut, and onto the top of the ridge. Here you can see out in all directions across open valleys and wooded ridges.

From the top of the ridge the road drops down into East Park Creek, through some open meadows flanked by lovely tall spruce. After crossing Park Creek and climbing a short hill past a gas pumping station, the road follows North Thompson Creek as far as Baylor Park, then bears south for 2 miles to Haystack Gate. From here you can bear right through the

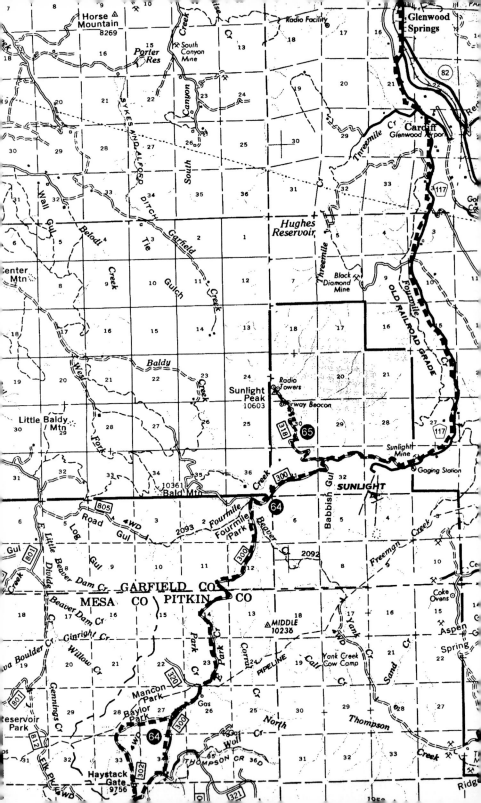

Haystack Gate (a gap in the hills) and circle around through Baylor Park on Forest Road 302 back to Road 300 for the return trip.

65. Sunlight Peak

Round Trip: 7 miles, 1–2 hours
Elevation Gain: 2,000'
Difficulty: Intermediate, Moderate/Strenuous
Map: p. 116

Notes: A sweet, mid-sized climb that takes you to the top of the highest peak in the Four Mile Park area, the Sunlight Peak route is good to do on its own or to cap a long training ride (31 miles round trip, 4,400' elevation gain) out from Glenwood Springs. Because of the road's southern exposure it dries out earlier and stays dry a little later in the season than most similar rides.

Access: (See Route #64). Sunlight Peak Road (Forest Road 318) branches right off Forest Road 300 two miles above its beginning at County Road 117; you can park in a large gravel lot another one-tenth mile up Road 300.

Route: Road 318 starts out a little steep and loose, then gentles out on a ½-mile run up along Four Mile Creek before switching back across the end of a ridge. There are a few steep spots and some nearly level stretches, but overall it's a steady, moderate climb switchbacking (14 times) up through the aspen forest and out into the meadows near the top of the mountain. Great views proliferate across Four Mile Park to the south and west. At the top, the road forks; the left fork goes up through a closed gate to service the electronic forest that stretches along the crest of the ridge. There's not much to see there and the electrical buzz of the transmission gear is enough to ruin the internal hum of a good workout. The right fork drops down and then out to a rocky point with a single radio tower and a spectacular view up the Roaring Fork Valley.

Cruising the jeep roads near Four Mile Park.

Index

A

Anaerobic Nightmare Trail, 45
Anthracite Creek, 102
Arbaney-Kittle Trail, 50-51
Arkansas River, 36
Arkansas Valley, 63
Around the Table, 56, 71, 74, 79
Ashcroft, 31, 33
Ashcroft Mountain, 32
Aspen, 11-13, 18-24, 27-29, 31, 33,
  35, 41, 43-46, 48, 54-55, 65,
  67-68, 81, 85, 90
Aspen Highlands, 41
Aspen Mountain, 11, 25, 27-29, 112
Assignation Ridge, 95
Avalanche Creek, 92

B

Bair Ranch, 107
Barnard Hut, 30
Basalt, 53-54, 56-57, 59, 61-62,
  67-69, 71, 74, 84, 87, 95
Basalt Bike Path, 54, 65, 67, 70
Basalt Mountain, 75, 79, 81, 83-84,
  86, 90, 95
Basalt Mountain Road, 76, 81, 83
Baylor Park, 115, 117
Bear Basin, 102
Bear Gulch, 113
Beaver Lake, 97
Benedict Bridge, 16, 19
Big Burn, 55
Boy Scout Trail, 110, 112-14
Braderich Creek Trail, 91
Brush Creek Cow Camp, 35
Brush Creek Valley, 40
Buck Creek, 104
Buck Creek Basin, 104
Burnt Mountain, 43, 45, 61
Burnt Mountain Loop, 60
Burnt Mountain Road, 59-60, 74
Buttermilk Ski Area, 11, 41, 43

C

Capitol Creek, 46, 53, 55, 67, 69-70
Capitol Creek Road, 53-55, 67, 70
Capitol Peak, 52, 55, 70, 92, 96
Carbondale, 53, 56, 65, 67-69, 75,
  77-79, 88, 90-91, 93-95, 97, 102
Castle Creek, 27-29, 31, 33
Castle Creek Road, 25, 27-29, 31, 33
Castle Peak, 33
Catherine Store, 71, 75, 77-79
Catherine Store Road, 71, 75-80
Cattle Creek, 71, 76, 78-81, 83-84
Cattle Creek Loop, 83
Cattle Creek Road, 76, 78-80
Chair Creek, 104
Chair Mountain, 104
Cherry Lake, 86
Coal Basin, 93
Colbran, 115
Collegiate Range, 31
Colorado Mountain College, 78
Colorado Plateau, 88
Colorado River, 105-7
Continental Divide, 29, 36, 61-62
Conundrum Creek, 27-28
Cottonwood Creek, 71, 80
Cottonwood Divide, 71, 80
Cottonwood Pass, 71, 76, 80, 85
Cottonwood Pass Road, 71, 79-80
Coulter Creek, 79
Coulter Creek Road, 71, 79-80
Cow Camp, 55
Crested Butte, 33, 35, 97, 99
Crested Butte Ski Area, 99
Crooked Creek, 59-60
Crooked Creek Pass, 59-60, 71, 74, 86
Crooked Creek Reservoir, 59-60, 74
(The) Crown, 94, 96
Crown Trails, 69, 88, 93-94
Crystal (City), 97-100
Crystal Mill, 98, 100
Crystal River, 88, 93, 98, 100, 102
Crystal River Valley, 81, 88
Crystal Springs/Cattle Creek Loop, 77

Crystal Springs Road, 78
Cunningham Creek, 64

D

Daggett Lane, 74
Daniels Hill, 97-98, 100
Dead Horse Mill, 98
Deep Creek, 104
Denver & Rio Grande Railroad, 11
Devil's Punchbowl, 97-99
Diemer Lake, 62, 65
Dinkle Lake, 68-70, 94
Dinkle Lake Road, 69
Divide (Snowmass Village), 44, 53-55
Divide Road, 37, 54
Dotsero, 106
Dry Park Road, 88, 90-91, 115

E

Eagle, 60
Eagle River Valley, 48, 56, 79
East Brush Creek, 35, 41, 60
East Coulter Creek, 71, 80
East Downey Creek, 86
East Park Creek, 115
East River, 35, 85, 99
East Snowmass Ditch Trail, 44
East Sopris Creek, 67
East Sopris Creek Divide, 67
East Sopris Creek Road, 53, 67-68
East Village, 44
El Jebel, 56, 71, 75-77, 79, 81, 94
El Jebel Road, 81
Elk Camp Road, 40, 44-45
Elk Mountain Ridge, 53, 55, 67
Elk Mountains, 13, 19, 22, 29, 78-79, 86
Elk Run, 54
Emerald Lake, 99
Emma, 67
Emma Road, 67-69
Erickson Lake, 86
Erickson Springs Campground, 102
Express Creek, 31-32
Express Creek Road, 31

F

Fat Tire Bike Week, 33
Fender Lane, 77
Flat Tops, 90-91, 95, 105, 109
Four Corners, 15-16, 19-23
Four Mile Creek, 110, 117
Four Mile Park, 91, 115, 117-18
Four Mile Park Road, 115
Four Mile Road, 91, 115
Frying Pan River, 50, 56, 59-60, 63, 71, 74
Frying Pan River Road, 56-57, 59-62, 64-65, 74, 86-87
Frying Pan River Trail, 63
Frying Pan Valley, 52, 56, 62-63, 65, 84

G

Garrett Peak, 55
Gates Hut, 61
Glendale Divide, 45
Glenwood Canyon, 90-91, 105, 112-13
Glenwood Canyon Bike Path, 60, 105-6
Glenwood Springs, 60, 75, 78-79, 88, 90-91, 105, 107, 109-10, 112-15, 117
Gold Hill, 29-30
Gothic, 99
Government Trail, 40-45, 55
Government Trail West, 41, 43-44
Grizzly, 106
Grizzly Creek, 35, 106
Grizzly Reservoir, 35-36
Gunnison Valley, 33
Gypsum, 71
Gypsum Creek, 71, 74, 86
Gypsum Creek Canyon, 74

H

Hagerman Pass, 56, 61-64
Hagerman Pass Road, 61, 64
Hagerman Tunnel, 63
Hanging Lake, 107
Hardscrabble Lake, 55
Hardscrabble Mountain, 71, 74
Hardscrabble Mountain Road, 74

Hay Park, 69-70, 88, 93
Hay Park Trail, 68-69, 94
Hayden Peak, 27-28
Haystack Gate, 115, 117
Haystack Mountain, 55
High Alpine Road, 40, 44
Highlands Peak, 28
Holland Hills, 65
Hooks Lane Bridge, 71
Horse Ranch, 38
Horseshoe Bend, 106
Hubbard Cave, 112-13
Hunter Creek, 13, 15-16, 18-19, 22
Hunter Creek Trail, 16, 18, 22
Hunter Creek Valley, 15-16, 18-19, 22
Hunter Valley Trail, 16, 18, 22
Hurricane Gulch, 29-30

I

Independence Pass, 50
Iowa Mine, 18
Iselin Park, 41
Ivanhoe Creek, 62
Ivanhoe Lake, 61, 63-64

J

Jerome Bar, 33
Jerome Park, 88, 90-91
Johnson/Silver Creek Trail, 50

K

Kebler Pass Road, 102, 104
Kobey Park, 48-50

L

Lake Ridge, 91, 93
Larkspur Mountain, 48-50
Last Chance Creek, 61
Lead King Basin, 88, 97-98, 100-1
Leadville, 61
Lenado, 20, 23, 46, 48, 50
Lenado Road, 23, 46
Lenado Loop, 19, 23-24
Lily Pad Lake, 63
Lime Creek, 57, 59-61
Lime Creek Canyon, 59
Lime Creek Road, 59-60
Lime Park, 59-61, 74

Lincoln Creek, 35
Lincoln Creek Campground, 35
Lincoln Creek Road, 35-36
Little Annie Basin, 27, 29
Little Annie Road, 25, 27-29, 31
Little Elk Creek, 67
Little Elk Creek Divide, 67
Lizard Lake, 98, 100
Lookout Mountain, 112-13
Lookout Mountain Road, 110, 112-13
Lookout Mountain Trail, 114
Lost Trail, 101
Lost Trail Creek, 97, 100
Lower River Road, 52-54, 65-67, 70
Lyle Lake, 61, 63-64

M

Mace Peak, 33
Marble, 97
Marcellina Mountain, 104
Margy's Hut, 49-50
Maroon Bells, 16, 20, 40, 102
Maroon Creek, 41, 43
Maroon Creek Road, 28, 31, 33, 43
McArthur Mountain, 30
McClure Pass, 97, 102
McLain Flats Road, 12, 20, 22
Meredith, 59, 74
Middle Brush Creek, 35
Middle Thompson Creek, 91
Midland Railroad, 61
Midnight Mine, 27
Midnight Mine Road, 25, 27-29
Missouri Heights, 71, 75-78, 80-81
Montezuma Basin, 33
Mosquito Range, 63
Mount Daly, 55
Mount Massive, 62-63
Mount Sopris, 13, 52-53, 55, 67-69,
     78, 81, 88, 90, 92-93, 96, 107, 109
Mt. Crested Butte, 99
Muddy Creek, 102
Mumsey Creek Road, 104

N

Nature Trail, 44
New York Creek, 35
New York Peak, 95

No Name, 106
No Name Canyon, 109
No Name Creek, 110, 11
North Fork Road, 61
North Thompson Creek, 91, 115

O

Old Snowmass, 65-66
Owl Creek, 41
Owl Creek bike path, 44-45
Owl Creek Road, 44-45, 55

P

Paonia, 115
Paonia Reservoir, 102
Park Creek, 115
Parsnip Flat, 92
Pearl Mountain, 34
Pearl Pass, 33
Pearl Pass Road, 33
platform, 13, 15
(The) Plunge, 19-20
Porcupine Loop, 88, 93-94
Porphyry Mountain, 50
Prince Creek Divide, 69, 96
Prince Creek Road, 68-69, 88, 93-96

Q

Queen's Gulch, 27

R

Ragged Mountain, 104
Ragged Mountain Trail, 88, 102
Raggeds, 104
Red Canyon Road, 79, 110, 112-13
Red Creek Road, 85-87
Red Creek Trail, 85
Red Mountain, 15-16, 18, 20-21, 48,
    109, 114
Red Mountain Road, 15, 107
Red Table Mountain, 50, 56, 59,
    74-75, 79, 81, 83-87, 90, 95
Red Table Radar Dome, 85-86
Red Table Road, 84-87
Redstone, 91, 93
Reservoir Bridge, 15-16, 18
Richmond Hill, 29, 31
Richmond Hill Road, 29-30

Richmond Ridge, 30
Ridge Trail, 45
Rim Trail, 37-38
Rio Grande Railroad, 24
Rio Grande Trail, 11-13, 20, 22-23,
    46, 54, 65
River Road, 46
Road 7, 67
Road 12, 102
Road 13, 80
Road 100, 71, 75, 77-79
Road 102, 77
Road 103, 48, 50, 78
Road 105, 61
Road 108, 88
Road 112, 78
Road 113, 71, 76, 78-80
Road 114, 112
Road 115, 79, 110, 113
Road 117, 115, 117
Road 120, 112-13
Road 121, 79-80
Road 122, 76
Road 125, 88, 91
Road 300, 115, 117
Road 302, 117
Road 305, 91
Road 306, 91
Road 307, 93
Road 311, 69
Road 318, 115, 117
Road 400, 74
Road 411, 74
Road 412, 74
Road 414, 60, 74
Road 425, 86
Road 502, 62, 65
Road 506, 60, 74
Road 508, 48-51
Road 509, 81, 83-84
Road 513, 51
Road 524, 81, 83
Road 526, 49-51
Road 532, 64
Road 602, 110
Road 898, 102
Roaring Fork River, 11-12, 16, 21, 23,
    35, 50, 53-54, 59, 69-70, 75, 85,
    105, 110

Rock Garden, 41, 43
Rocky Fork Creek, 50-52, 87
Ruby, 35-36
Ruedi Creek Road, 86
Ruedi Dam, 56, 86-87
Ruedi Reservoir, 59, 74, 87
Ruedi Trail, 84-87

S

San Juan Mountains, 33
Savage Peak, 61
Sawatch Range, 33, 50, 59, 112
Schofield, 99
Schofield Park, 99
Schofield Pass, 88, 97
Schofield Pass Road, 97
Sellar Lake, 62, 65
Sellar Park, 61-62, 64-65
Sellar Peak, 62
Sellar Peak Road, 62-64
Seven Castles, 57
Shadyside Trail, 21
Shippee's Draw, 71, 80
Shoshone, 106-7
Silt, 115
Silver Creek, 48, 50
Ski Sunlight, 91
Slaughterhouse Bridge, 11-13, 22, 24
Slim Jim Gulch, 61
Smuggler/Hunter Creek Loop, 13, 18
Smuggler Mine, 13
Smuggler Mountain, 13, 15, 18, 81
Smuggler Mountain Road, 13-15, 18
Snodgrass Mountain, 99
Snowmass Creek, 38, 46, 53-55
Snowmass Creek Road, 53-55, 66-67, 70
Snowmass General Store, 53-55, 66-67
Snowmass Mountain, 102
Snowmass Ski Area, 40-41, 43, 45, 95
Snowmass Village, 37-38, 43-45, 53-55, 85
Sopris Creek Road, 67-68
South Branch Road, 91
South Thompson Creek Trail, 91-92
Spring Creek, 59
Spring Gulch Divide, 71

Spring Gulch ski trails, 88, 91
Spring Park, 76
Spring Park Reservoir, 76, 81
Spring Valley, 78, 110, 112
Spring Valley Loop, 78
Spring Valley Road, 112
Stony Ridge, 91
Storm King Mountain, 113
Sugarloaf, 86
Summer Road, 25, 27-28
Sundeck, 27-29
Sunlight Peak, 95, 112, 115, 117
Sunlight Peak Road, 117
Sunlight Ski Area, 115
Sunnyside Trail, 19-22
Sweet Hill, 88
Sylvan Lake, 60, 71, 74

T

Tabor Creek, 35
Tagert Hut, 33
Tall Pines, 88, 91-92
Taylor Creek Road, 84
Taylor Lake, 31
Taylor Pass, 29, 31
Taylor Pass Road, 29, 31
Taylor River Valley, 31
Tenth Mountain Bridge, 16, 18-19
Tenth Mountain Trail, 49-50
Thomas Lakes, 69-70
Thomasville, 56-57, 59, 71, 74
Thompson Creek Road, 88, 91
Tiehack Ski Area, 43
Toklat Lodge, 31
Toner Reservoir, 83
Trail 1909, 81, 83-87
Trail 1952, 92
Trail 1957, 69
Trail 1984, 48
Trail 1989, 23, 46
Transfer Trail, 109
Treasure Mountain, 100
Triangle Peak, 50, 52
Truro Creek, 35
Two Creeks Trail, 44-45
Two Rivers Park, 105, 107
Two Rivers Road, 65, 67, 71

U

Upper Cattle Creek Road, 71, 75-77, 80-81
Upper River Road, 52-54

V

Valley Road, 71, 74-75
Van Horn Park, 16, 19-22

W

Warren Lakes, 13-15
Watson Divide, 53
Watson Divide Road, 53-54
Weller Lake Campground, 35
West Brush Creek Road, 74
West Brush Creek Valley, 60
West Elks, 104
West Sopris Creek, 68, 70, 93
West Sopris Creek Road, 67-69, 94-95
West Willow Creek, 40
Whitehorse Springs, 12
Whites Lake, 43
Wilbur Creek, 48
Williams Creek Reservoir, 104
Williams Mountains, 19, 22, 50, 95
Williams Peak, 115
Willits Lane, 71
Willow Park, 91
Wilson/Green Hut, 33
Wilton Jaffee Park, 12, 23
Windy Point, 109-10
Wood Road, 40-41, 44
Woody Creek, 11-12, 23, 46, 48, 50-51, 53, 65-66
Woody Creek Bridge, 12
Woody Creek Road, 23, 46
Woody Creek Tavern, 11-12, 23, 46, 48, 52
Woody Creek Trail, 48

Y

Yeoman Park Road, 60